PRAYERS OF THE PROVERBS 31 WOMAN

The Prayer Book for Feminine Wives and Wives-to-be

31 Days Prayers & Affirmations for Yourself, Your Husband and Children

Swabrina Love

Prayers Of The Proverbs 31 Woman

The Prayer Book for Feminine Wives and Wives-to-be

31 Days Prayers & Affirmations for Yourself, Your Husband and Children

© Copyright 2021 by Swabrina Love

ISBN number –

Paperback   978-1-8381888-2-5
Hard cover 978-1-8381888-3-2
Audio   978-1-8381888-1-8

Printed in the United Kingdom
Independently Published

For bulk orders please contact info@myproverbs31family.com
for a generous discount schedule.

ACKNOWLEDGEMENT

I will like to express my thanks first and foremost to my Love, Lord and Saviour Jesus Christ. He uses the most unlikely and weakest people to do great things. I am in awe that he will use me to produce this life changing book and ministry. It is all by HIS grace. Writing this book did not come without its fair share of battles, but I thank the Holy Spirit for his grace, strength and inspiration and for allowing me to grow through the process of writing.

Quick shout outs to some very important people the Lord used to support me before and during the process of writing. Thanks to prophet Cynthia, Reverend Israel and Bishop Tuffour whose prophetic utterances stirred up the gift of writing in me. Prophet Cynthia spoke about my book without knowing me even before I ever dreamt about writing a book. I speak about how the Lord used Rev Israel and Bishop Tuffour in the book.

To my Proverbs31 community, thank you for your support and encouragement to start out the ministry during the pandemic. This book was birthed during our prayer meetings! Thank you Dell, Lola, Michelle, and all the beautiful ladies on my launch team and P31 community for your continued support, celebration, and encouragement.

Thanks to my friends Emelia and Emete, who were a source of wisdom and listening ear through the complex logistics of publishing this book the first year.

To my coach and mentor, Chengi Tobun you are a God sent in wisdom and in character. Thank you for believing in me, seeing me and honouring me. I learnt a lot from you most especially in my feminine walk and in coaching! Thank you for your counsel, push and encouragement during the times I felt alone and wanted to give up.

MY FREE GIFT TO YOU

As a way of saying thank you for purchasing this book, I am offering you my Master Class on How to Meet, Magnetise and Marry your Purpose and Legacy Partner in 90 Days Without the Frustrations of Endless Dating or Compromising Your Faith or Values, and a few extra bonuses mentioned in this book.

Jump on the link and access the bonuses at www.myproverbs31family.com/POP31bonuses. See you on the other side!

Table of Content

SECTION 1

PRAYERS FOR YOUR FEMININITY

Day 1

A CALL FOR PRAYERS AMID DESPAIR

The LORD is close to the broken-hearted and saves those who are crushed in spirit.

-Psalm 34:18

In 2018, I expected to get engaged and it was going to be one of the best years of my life. I felt it in my stomach! I was so excited and expectant.

The previous year, I received breakthroughs in many areas which I had been praying about for a long time. As a result, I finally felt ready and in a good place to embark on a relationship leading to marriage.

I refer to this period of my life as my 'Passover season'. Passover is a Jewish celebration to mark their emancipation from 400 years of slavery in Egypt. They experienced a lot of miracles during Passover year and were freed from Egypt to accomplish their dreams in a new and prosperous country of their own, as God had promised them.

To my surprise, however, 2018 took a quick turn and my excitement at the end of the 2017 quickly turned into disappointment and despair. I sank into a depression that lasted many months. Externally I was in a better place than I had ever been. Just like the Jewish people I was freed from many 'slavery' circumstances which I faced for many years, but the turmoil happening inside of me didn't match my external reality. My mind felt like it was slowly deteriorating and I was gradually losing myself and my personality. The best way to describe my experience is that my chest area literally felt shattered into many broken pieces and was being held together by sellotape. I felt disconnected from my body and it seemed like I was looking down on the world from the sky. I was regularly in tears sometimes even in public spaces. I was having a mental meltdown!

Faced with my internal reality for many months, I came to a realisation that I may never be well enough again to attract or keep love, let alone get married. I then began to make peace with a new reality of being single forever.

My experience mirrored that of the Jewish people during their emancipation from slavery. Elation quickly turned into misery. After leaving Egypt, the place of slavery, they came into the wilderness where they were confronted with a lot of unexpected challenges and battles on their way to their promised land. The wilderness was that 'in between' place from freedom to manifestation of their hopes and dreams. Unbeknown to them, their journey through the wilderness was a place where they had to face and heal their emotional wounds, traumas, torture, mindset, behaviours and attitudes from 400 years of slavery. They needed to fight a few more battles internally and externally before the manifestation of their dreams and prophetic promise.

In my wilderness season, God made it clear to me in many ways that He was with me. One day I was in church, deep in prayer, asking God to take the depression away and restore my vibrant personality. I prayed quietly, with tears flooding down my face. Soon after, Rev Israel began to give a prophetic word from the pulpit. He said, "There is someone who has been going through what seems like a depression. The Lord said you are not going through a mental breakdown but a pruning (healing)." He also prophesied that he saw the person in a wedding gown. What a timely word! Just a couple of hours earlier I had resolved to start adjusting my mind to being single forever. This prophetic encounter was the medicine my soul needed to start gradually healing!

It turned out that what I felt was a mental health decline was actually a 'wilderness' process of healing and pruning in preparation for getting me ready for my marriage promise.

The wilderness process can truly be painful but is necessary, not only for change and hope, but for purpose, capacity and growth. Many of the conversations and revelations that I received from the Lord during this

3

painful period of my life carried the message and tools God gave me to share in this book and in my coaching programmes and courses around healing, purpose, marriage, breaking curses, entrepreneurship, and creating a renewed generational legacy.

The Lord laid a strong call in my heart for women to begin praying for their husbands and men at large. He told me that many very high-value, godly, and consecrated women will remain single, not by God's will but because of the state of men at large.

Our Prayers are therefore, needed to help activate not only our husbands but men at large to become kings worthy of God's high-priced daughters. This prompting in my spirit was confirmed by three other women, who urgently called for Prayers for men and families at the same time.

Furthermore, women need to heal themselves and also support men to heal through the power of Prayers, femininity, influence and other strategies that will be taught throughout this book.

This book is a call for both married and single women to pray, and take the necessary actions to become the feminine purposeful wives God called them to be and in so doing, manifest their homes and families for purpose, love and legacy.

Sis, you may be in despair or tried everything and have ultimately lost hope where marriage and family is concerned. I want to encourage you. Even in your despair, God can infuse hope and strength into your inner being. If you are in an unhappy place in your marriage, your single season, or as a parent and are intentional about making a positive change, I highly recommend that you give the supernatural a try, through participating in this 31-day prayer challenge. You will begin to hope again, dream again and manifest the marriage and family that God intended for you to have.

Our case study for wifeliness and femininity throughout this book will be drawn from the 'Proverbs 31 lady'[1] and Queen Esther in the Bible.

---

[1] "Proverbs 31 woman" is a common term among Christian circles used to refer to the ideal character of a king's or high value man's wife

4

The excellent wife in Proverbs 31 was an awesome all-rounder known for her exceptional ability to balance womanhood, character, family, business and beauty. Most people see the woman described in Proverbs 31, as a superwoman whose standard is unattainable for the modern woman. However, she is the perfect definition of a feminine wife, a standard of womanhood that can be attained with God's help through Prayers, and through intentional efforts to grow, become, influence and manifest femininity.

To help you manifest and embody the principles that will taught over the next 31 days, we will be employing a three-step process: (1) write your vision, (2) pray and (3) take action:

(1) Write the vision down and make it Clear[2]
Visualisation and scripting—the art of imagining and writing down your goals, plans and desires —are proven methods for manifestation attested in both biblical and secular world views. There is space in this book for you to write down your vision, purpose, desires and expectations around family and marriage. Setting your expectation from the start of this adventure will not only help you have goals and visions to work with, but will enable you to pray with hope, faith and expectation.

(2) Pray
The transformative power of Prayers and affirmative words has also been widely attested to through historical and modern accounts. You can embark on the next 31 days of Prayers alone or with a group of like-minded people. Working with a partner or a group will help you be accountable. There is also manifestation power in agreement. A scripture from the Bible says "If two or more of you shall agree a thing, it shall be established."[3]

You're welcome to join my prayer community on Facebook—My Proverbs 31 Family. We take part in various prayer and growth challenges throughout the year related to femininity, purpose, healing, marriage, men, children and family.

---

[2] Bible, Habakkuk 2:2
[3] Bible, Matthew 18:19

(3) Take Action

While there is miraculous power in Prayers, it is not an excuse to do nothing, but rather should be the propellant to take actions that yield extraordinary results. In fact, the Bible reprimands a person who responds to a practical need by praying only by stating that 'faith without works is dead'[4]—meaning Prayers without corresponding actions are ineffective, while Prayers with corresponding action are necessary for manifestation.

Prayer is a two-way communication where we pray to God, but also take time aside to listen, journal and obey any instruction or direction that follows. After each section in this book, there is space to listen, journal and plan actions as it relates to manifesting your goals and desires for your family.

Sometimes the appropriate action might be to pray, to rest, trust or do something else. All the same, as you work through the Prayers in this book, your spiritual antenna will be on and you will hear God's direction more clearly, as He downloads encouragement and strategies in relation to yourself and your family.

The women who engage in my marriage preparation coaching programme and other Proverbs 31 events are supported to take action and apply strategies that will help them transform and prepare to attract their purpose marriage. I invite you to attend my **FREE Purpose Marriage Preparation masterclass** [5]which delves deeper into the SPARC method for proactively preparing for and manifesting your purpose marriage. (SPARC stands for self love, Purpose, Attraction and Femininity and Cycles, Curses and Character).

---

[4] Bible, James 2:14-17
[5] www.myproverbs31family.com/POP31bonuses

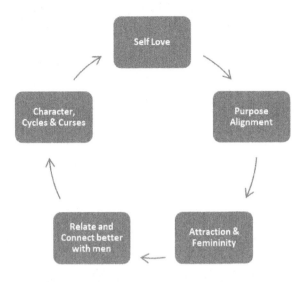

Why a Prayer Book?

Prayer is one of the most powerful methods that I and many others have experienced for change and transformation, especially for dire situations when all other practical methods failed to yield desired results.

As humans with a loving Creator, though we have been given the option to choose God, we were NOT designed to go through life independent of God. God is a loving Father who is interested in the affairs of His children. He desires a relationship with His children through prayer which is a primary way of establishing communication between God and man. So, as well as being a means of communication and relationship, prayer is a way of getting God involved in our affairs.

Secondly, life is multidimensional and consists of the seen and unseen world. Science proves that a lot of activity that is invisible to the naked eye underpins what we see, hear or feel. For example, for sound to be audible or television visible, there are underlying radioactivity and interactions that occur which are invisible to the naked eye. Likewise, underpinning the physical world— what we see, hear, smell or experience physically—is a very active spiritual world also known as the supernatural. Prayer is a way of influencing and shifting things in the spiritual world by invoking the supernatural power of God to produce results or manifestation into the physical realm. Affirmations said during Prayers are very effective for transformation in our minds and our world.

The fight for Godly and happy families occurs in the three dimensions of life—the spirit, the soul and the physical realm. The enemy of your life, who is a spiritual being, will fight to break your family because families are the foundation of a healthy society and the structure through which God dispenses many of his blessings to his creation. Prayer is a means by which we can engage the spiritual and win the spiritual battles for our marriage, which will in turn affect our psychological and physical world.

Finally, prayer is an act of humility.

When we pray, we are declaring our need for God. We take off our pride, independence and self-sufficiency and are humble enough to acknowledge our dependence on God. Just like a good husband wouldn't want his wife making important decisions independently, God wants us to acknowledge him in our quest for a happy marriage rather than live our lives independently of him. God rewards us with direction, purpose, strength and manifestation when we trust and invite him into our affairs including our relationships, marriage, parenting and other aspects of life.

In summary, this prayer book is for you if you desire a purpose- driven marriage and are intentional about raising your self-worth, healing and becoming the feminine woman God called you to be. If you have tried all the methods you know, to have the marriage of your dreams, but to no avail, this book is for you.

This life changing book is also for you if you have a family but are facing challenges either with your spouse or with your children and need help. God says, "Call on me in times of trouble and I will answer you, I will deliver you."[6] The psalmist says, "Oh taste and see that the Lord is good."[7] If you are single, there is no better time to start preparing for your purpose marriage through Prayers and corresponding action. This book will help you do that!

---

[6] Bible, Psalm 50:15
[7] Bible, Psalm 34:18

As you embark on this 31-day prayer challenge, you will taste of God's goodness in your home in a new way. I look forward to hearing your testimonials!

So tell me, what do you hope to achieve as you embark on the next 31 days? Please write it down on the next page.

Day 2

WRITE THE VISION DOWN

My goals and desires for myself, my spouse, and children as I embark on the next 31 days are:

Day 3

FIRE UP YOUR FEMININITY

Many daughters have done well, But you excel them all..

-Proverbs 31:29

While deciding on the title of this book, I came across some people who asked me about femininity. One person asked, *'aren't all wives feminine?'*

'How can you put the Proverbs 31 and femininity in the same sentence since she was anything but feminine. In fact she was intimidating,' another person asked.

These questions led me to include a chapter to clarify and explain any misconceptions around the word femininity.

Femininity, is best explained by studying the functional differences between the female reproductive system and that of their male counterparts. For example, during the reproductive cycle, the male donates millions of sperms which all swim towards, and compete to fertilise one female egg. Furthermore, evolutionary science teaches that in ancient times men's primary roles were to protect and hunt prey so as to provide for their families, while women were referred to as gatherers, who primarily gathered food from plants, and looked after the home and children.

In the same vain, femininity can therefore, be described as a state of being rested, receiving, open, free, pursued, protected and taking less risk, while masculinity is best described as the state of providing, pursuing, chasing, hustling, hunting, being competitive, generous, protective and taking greater risk for the family.

Furthermore, femininity can be also seen as the state of being playful, dainty, soft, attractive, vulnerable and open to masculine protection and cherishing, as opposed to being strong and independent.

Whilst femininity is traditionally associated with women and masculinity with men, it isn't necessarily an exclusive description of any gender as both men and women can and do possess feminine and masculine traits. Hence, the term masculine and feminine is used to describe a person's disposition or predominant state, as opposed to their exclusive state. So, a healthy feminine woman will inevitably sometimes display masculine traits although her predominant state is feminine. The same for a healthy masculine man- he will at times have a feminine side to him, although this isn't his dominant trait.

Women have traditionally and naturally displayed more feminine characteristics, while men exhibit more masculine characteristics. However, in modern society this is less the case. Women are increasingly displaying more independence and masculine traits, while the tendency of some men, is to be more in their feminine than masculine side.

In summary, table below describes feminine versus masculine traits in women.

Which traits describe you and what is your predominant energy or way of being?

Feminine traits	Masculine traits
Soft, sensual, gentle, dainty and delicate	Strong, harsh, independent, and protecting
Quiet, calm, peaceful, serene	Loud, noisy, argumentative, dramatic
Open and vulnerable	Closed, strong, independent, capable, guarded, suspecting
Open and available to be loved, desired, and pursued	Pursues, does, woos, closed and unavailable for masculine pursuit
Playful, jovial, flirtatious, happy, laughs	Takes life too seriously
Receives, appreciates, asks for help and makes time for self-care and pampering	Gives, sacrificial, selfless, self-sufficient and doesn't like to receive or ask for help
Emotional, intuitive, and able to connect deeply	Closed, guarded, suspicious and doesn't like to open or share emotionally
Nurturing and caring	Mothering and controlling
Trusting, restful, leant back, and makes space	Hustles, chases, and controlling
Submissive, respectful, and facilitating of masculine leadership	Leads, emasculates, controls, competitive, stubborn and unyielding
Humble, flexible, agreeable and teachable	Egoistic, stubborn, argumentative and insists on being right and having things her way

Feminine traits	Masculine traits
Creative, able to give life and birth ideas, dreams, businesses, and babies	Works hard, hustles, always busy, workaholic, unproductive, no time for creativity, play or connection
Works smarter and gets more done with ease	Works hard, hustles, busy and struggles
Provides support, help, influence, peace, respect, beauty, creativity, play, order, enjoyment, colour, encouragement, and admiration	Provides leadership, protection, finances, direction, sacrificial love and direction
Attractive, desirable, and magnetic to the masculine	**Repelling to and competitive with the masculine. Attractive to the feminine**
Influential and inspiring of masculine provision and protection	**Inspires competition, clash and neglect from the masculine**

So why a prayerbook for feminine wives and wives to be?

Firstly, it's important to acknowledge the necessity of the masculine side of a woman such as her ability to work, lead, mother, plan, pursue, give, work, struggle, suffer and hustle. These are all necessary traits to be applauded in women. The challenge though is that modern day society and feminism have led women to be predominantly in their masculine energy of hustling, pursuing and leading, and unable to tap into their feminine way of being. This poses a lot of issues in relationships, and is especially a problem for a woman who desires to be, or is coupled with a masculine man, who is a leader, provider, protector, pursuer, doer, 'wooer' and 'hustler' in the relationship. Subsequently, many women in my world complain about men in their lives either as suitors or husbands, who are overly feminine, not driven, unprotective and stingy. These men expect their women to exhibit the masculine traits and take up the provider, protector, pursuer and hustler role in the relationship. As a result, it becomes very difficult for the woman to respect their feminine husbands or boyfriends.

Secondly many women at their core are wired to be happiest and most productive, especially in relationships, when they are predominantly in their feminine rested essence. Modern circumstances have made it increasingly difficult for women to be in their feminine essence, hence the default state of women, seems to be their masculine side. This has a negative impact on her mental and physiological health, sexual drive and hormone balance. This also leads to friction in relationships as it then becomes harder for the woman to offer respect, admiration, adoration or sex to her husband.

Thirdly, marriages and relationships thrive when there is masculine and feminine polarity where one person (either the man or the woman) mostly takes up the masculine position and the other person, the more feminine role in a relationship.

The law of polarity shows how opposite energies attract and how things exist in duals. For example, in science positively charged atoms attract negatively charged atoms while atoms that have the same charge repel one another. We see that in other areas where opposite attracts, pair up and co-exist, such as male and female, love and hate, sadness and joy. Tony Robinson describes polarity in relationships as "the spark that occurs between two opposing energies." He goes on to say that for a relationship to work and be passionate, "one partner has to provide the masculine energy while the other brings the feminine."

There is friction in the relationship when both parties take up or compete for the masculine or feminine position or take up positions that are opposed to their natural dispositions.

Do you find yourself in friction with men, who seem as if they are running away from you? Or do you only seem to attract feminine men in your relationships and friendships who want to take from you, are not protective of you, are stingy or competitive with you? Perhaps you are overly leaning into your masculine energy and are displaying traits described on the righthand side of the table above, which will inevitably cause masculine men to be repelled from you, and feminine men to be attracted to you.

In summary, if you already have a masculine man or desire a man, who loves, leads, provides, cherishes, and protects his woman—you must learn to intentionally tone down your masculinity and raise up your feminine essence when relating with your man. This is because embracing more of your feminine side not only causes masculine men to be attracted to you, but also inspires your partner to take up the masculine role in the relationship of loving, providing, pursuing, protecting and doing for you.

With training and intentionality, you can be successful at work or business while still balancing your femininity at home. In fact, this ability is the advantage of the modern woman. You can have the best of both worlds, but you must first believe and choose to work at it.

Despite having a business and juggling so many leadership roles, the Proverbs 31 woman still knew how to apply her feminine nature at home by respecting, nurturing, and catering to her husband's needs as well as the family. I go in-depth into how she does this in later chapters in this book.

Even though we are speaking about femininity in the context of marriage and relationship, femininity and masculinity dynamics applies to multiple areas of life including your attitude and relationships with God, family, friends, colleagues, acquaintances and strangers.

The aim of this book is not to ask you to give up all the masculine aspects of your personality, but to encourage you to embrace more of your feminine essence, especially in your relationships. I have taken a U-turn for the better, since I learnt to raise my feminine traits and tone down my masculine traits in some areas of my life. This is also the testimony of many women who have consciously put in the extra effort to embrace their femininity and have been rewarded with life- changing results in their lives, work, businesses and relationships. Do a YouTube search on femininity and listen to thousands of femininity transformation stories.

In my proverbs 31 community, we go deeper and learn how to practice and embody femininity in every area of life.

Let us pray:

SCRIPTURE RECITATION

The heart of her husband trusts in her, and he will have no lack of gain. She does him good, and not harm, all the days of her life.

PROVERBS 31:11

Submit to one another. For wives, this means submit to your husbands as to the Lord

EPHESIANS 5:21-22

Let it be [the inner beauty of] the hidden person of the heart, with the imperishable quality and unfading charm of a gentle and peaceful spirit, [one that is calm and self-controlled, not overanxious, but serene and spiritually mature] which is very precious in the sight of God.

1 PETER 3:4

Love is not rude. It does not insist on its own way; it is not irritable or resentful;

1 CORINTHIANS 13:5

But the wisdom from above is first of all pure. It is also peace loving, gentle always, and willing to yield to others. It is full of mercy and the fruit of good deeds. It shows no favoritism and is always sincere.

JAMES 3:17

Be still, and know that I am God! I will be honored by every nation. I will be honored throughout the world.

PSALM 46:10

Prayers

1. Lord, beautify me from the inside out. Let me be attractive on the outside, and internally in my character and femininity.

2. I receive the wisdom to be more feminine— soft, submissive and open to receive love and godly leadership with an open heart.

3. I am worthy of love and pursuit and I will be sought after, pursued and prized highly by my husband, children, friends, family and the world at large.

4. I am pursued, loved and cherished by high quality men, including family members, colleagues, friends and acquaintances.

5. I attract masculine men in my life whose joy is to serve, protect and provide for me

6. Help me, Lord to be trusting, believing, relaxed, receiving and open to my husband's love and leadership.

7. I give back to the masculine in my life (especially my husband) with respect, love, peace, appreciation, and submission.

8. Grant me wisdom to be peaceful, peacemaking, easy to get along with, forgiving, receptive, submissive, teachable, able to deescalate quarrels, empowering and encouraging to my husband and those around me.

9. I am soft, submissive and open to receive love, pursuit and godly leadership with an open heart.

10. I carry an aura of laughter, playfulness, excitement and joy everywhere I go.

11. Give me the wisdom to connect with my man's heart, excite his emotions and keep his trust.

12. May I be protective and caring for his heart and not do or say anything that will betray him.

13. I apply tact and femininity even when I feel upset.

14. Help me to do my husband good all the days of my life.

15. I exercise self-control and self-restraint, so that I can always show goodness and kindness, even when I feel upset.

16. I grow in godly character—love, joy, peace, patience, kindness, gentleness, goodness, faithfulness, and self- discipline.

17. Help me to grow in love —the love that is patient, kind and gentle, not easily offended, agreeable, forgives easily, keeps no record of wrong, trusting, patient and is tolerant.

18. Take away excessive masculinity from my personality. Remove— pride, selfishness, stubbornness, anger, laziness, control and competitiveness.

19. Thank you for the blood of Jesus that washes me and cleanses all flaws that get in the way of my femininity and wifely character.

Day 4

SELF WORTH, SELF LOVE AND IDENTITY

A truly good wife is the most precious treasure a man can find! She is more precious than jewels, and nothing you desire can compare with her.

-Proverbs 31:10

As a woman, you are a powerful force to be reckoned with. Your greatest superpowers lie within your virtues—your character, femininity, sexuality, influence, gifts, talents, and productivity.

Women are the biggest influencers of culture and have the power to give life either through their womb's miraculous ability to receive sperm, nurture it, and turn into a whole baby pushed into the world, or your power to take a small idea, nurture it, and turn it into a tangible product, project or business venture. You bring so much colour, creativity and beauty to the world.

Despite all these virtues you possess as a woman, without an awareness of your worth and value, all your virtues will lie dormant.

Many amazing, successful, and beautiful women settle for mediocre marriages and relationships because they don't know their worth or how to place appropriate value or price on their worth. Sis, your awareness of your own value and an ability to place a worthy price around your value, is the key to unlock the many superpowers in you which may currently be hidden.

In fact, your success in life and relationships is proportional to the value you place on yourself, time and commitment. This is why some of the most beautiful, kindest, and most generous women attract very abusive relationships due to low self-esteem and the belief that they can't get or deserve any better.

Your worth as a woman is often hidden amid low self-esteem, bad experiences, poor character, rejection, childhood trauma, bad relationships, rape, abuse, neglect, and negative life experiences.

Just like Tamar in the Bible[8] who was so desirable and beautiful, but remained depressed, unwanted, and alone after being raped by her brother, many women are in a state of desolation, depression, and dejection because of what they have been through. Some, unfortunately, never recover from the abuse and trauma they went through.

Your worth is not dependent on your past or present negative experiences, who people say you are, your marital status, or whether you have children. You are far more precious than the priciest jewel. God intentionally made you for a great purpose and deposited in you many unique qualities, gifts and talents to demonstrate His glory. My message for you, dear daughters of God, is to break free from your traumatic past, present experiences, or what people or society say about you. Come out of your grave, unlock the prison gates, take off the sheets of shame, sadness and self-loathing.

Here are three keys you can use to unlock your worth and break free from the events and traumas that have kept you covered.

1. Believe

Beauty, you are so precious, valuable, and needed. You are priced higher than the universe by the God who created the universe. If only you would believe it.

Sometimes, you continually experience and tolerate disrespect, abuse, being walked all over, being used and abused because you don't know who you are. It is therefore crucial that you get acquainted with your greatness, worth, value, uniqueness, gifts, talents, purpose, and character. Here are a few ways to believe:

---

[8] Bible, 2 Samuel 13.

- **Discover your worth.** Ask God to open your eyes to your strength and create scenarios and friendships that allow you to see your greatness. Repeat the Prayers in this chapter and/or book many times and watch the way you see yourself and the way the world values you begin to elevate. Even your quirks, insecurities, and challenges can add value to you and the world around you, if only you would believe it. You also discover and uncover your worth through in-depth healing work. We go in-depth into how to heal in subsequent chapters.

- **Speak it.** Write your strengths down and tell yourself about your worth frequently. Words are very powerful in readjusting your mindset. When negative thoughts, circumstances, and people around you challenge your value, the words you speak to yourself, makes all the difference. You must not succumb to the internal or external voices that lie about your value. For me, reciting and playing back God's words and songs about my worth from the Bible to myself has made a huge difference in helping me heal from past trauma.

- **Upgrade your friendships.** Intentionally surround yourself with people who see and respect your worth, and separate from people who don't. The same goes for workplaces, church, or social groups. Address dishonour or walk away from communities that don't value and appreciate your worth. People who use, abuse, and disrespect you need to go from your inner circle, to make room for better people.

2.   Display your worth

Come out of hiding and begin to shine. You've been hiding long enough behind fear, insecurities, and low confidence. The time has come for you to show up and shine in your beautiful gifts and talents. Now is the time to unveil and turn up in your glory. Daughter of God, you have been created and gifted to bless the world. How can you be a blessing when you are in hiding? I pray that you tear off the sheets, come out of your hiding, arise from your depression, and begin to shine in all your splendors.

Displaying your worth includes:

- Putting effort into your mental health, self-care and appearance

- Being kind and generous to those in need
- Doing a passion project that serves and influences others
- Branding, and selling products and services that solve problems or meet needs
- Working on and using your gifts and talents to serve others
- Increasing your visibility by speaking up, sharing your ideas, strategies, message, and service offline or online

I pray that the Lord will give you courage, direction, and ideas on how you can display your worth for those who would benefit from and value it.

3.   Put a price on it

Knowing your worth doesn't always mean that you will not encounter people who will seek to diminish, disrespect, use, abuse, and insult you, like you are worth nothing. So, in addition to knowing your worth, you must be skilled and confident to place a price, standard and boundary on your worth, your time, friendship, and gifts, and communicate this price. You must no longer allow people to easily take you for granted, toss you about, use and abuse you, or disrespect you when they feel like it.

- Decide the price for your time, attention, and service—this can include monetary or non-monetary value such as respect, mutuality, and appreciation.
- Tactfully and lovingly communicate your price, requirements, and boundaries when breached.
- Separate from and limit access to people who repeatedly disrespect your boundaries after you have communicated to them.

In my marriage preparation course and coaching programme, I help women identify, shine and profit in their purpose as well as practice setting healthy boundaries in love and relationship.

I pray for God's special grace, wisdom, and ease for you to communicate your boundaries in love and stick with them. I pray the Lord places you in environments where you are honoured and respected, just as God honours and values you. Let us pray:

Scripture Recitation

Because you are precious in my eyes and honoured, and I love you, I give men in return for you, peoples in exchange for your life.

ISAIAH 43:2

Arise [from spiritual depression to a new life], shine [be radiant with the glory and brilliance of the LORD]; for your light has come, And the glory and brilliance of the LORD has risen upon you.

ISAIAH 60:1

Neither do people light a lamp and put it under a basket. Instead, they set it on a stand, and it gives light to everyone in the house. In the same way, let your light shine before men, that they may see your good deeds and glorify your Father in heaven.

MATTHEW 5:15- 16

Prayers

1. Thank you, Lord, for honouring, loving, and respecting me and placing so much value in me.

2. Thank you that I am God's precious and high-priced treasure. My value is high, more than money can buy.

3. Help me to see and love myself as You made me— precious, high value, high worth, beautiful, desirable, a gift, royalty.

4. I am the most beautiful person I know on the inside and on the outside.

5. I am beautifully, fearfully, wonderfully, and intentionally crafted by God for a good purpose.

6. I have outstanding character and carry an enchanting and joyful presence that adds value everywhere I go.

7. My character is beautiful, warm, and inviting.

8. I have a quiet, soothing, and gentle spirit, and I exhibit strength with meekness, humility, and influence.

9. I radiate joy, laughter, playfulness, femininity, and sunshine wherever I go.

10. Lord, heal me from past, present, and future hurt and pain that covers my worth.

11. Deliver me from abuse, neglect, shame, anxiety, depression, rejection, and trauma [state your specific experience].

12. Remove the veil of negative words and experiences, low self-esteem, rejection, and shame, and show me who I really am.

13. Help me to overcome every mindset or character in me that does not reflect your beauty and confidence.

14. I arise, break forth, break out, shine, and radiate God's love and light to others.

15. I am no longer covered and hidden by shame, rejection, low self-esteem, or abuse.

16. I am raised from weakness to strength, from dishonour to honour, low self-esteem to confidence.

17. I tear off the grave cloths of low self-esteem, self-hate and rejection, and I put on the garment of splendour, beauty, glory, and righteousness.

18. I am honoured, appreciated, and celebrated.

19. The Lord is restoring double honour for every shame, rejection and abuse I experienced.

20. I have been bought with a high price by God's precious son, Yeshua Christos, so I demand a price of respect and honour on my time, friendships, and service.

21. I set healthy boundaries and standards in all my relationships and receive wisdom on how to communicate my boundaries kindly and effectively.

22. My value increases daily, and I am sought after, pursued, celebrated, and honoured.

23. I am valued highly. A high price and reward is placed on my character, my time, experiences, counsel, gifts, products, service, ideas, and creativity.

24. Today is the last day that I will be treated like a doormat for people to trample over.

25. I attract people who see, encourage, value, honour, and respect my worth as I do theirs.

26. I separate from people and environments that don't value or cultivate my greatness with honour and respect.

27. I am worthy of love and pursuit, and I will be sought after, pursued, and prized highly by my husband, children, friends, family, communities, and the world at large.

Day 5

FEMININE INFLUENCE

Men listened to me and waited and kept silence for my counsel. After I spoke, they did not speak again, and my word dropped upon them.

-Job 29:21–25

A woman's biggest superpower is in her ability to influence. A wife who maximises this innate ability can influence her husband, children, friends, family, and even strangers in positions of power and authority. In my culture men are commonly described as the head of the home, while women are the neck that controls the head. The "neck" position, the position of influence, is a privileged and powerful position that women have been utilising from the beginning of time. As my mentor commonly says, "women are the custodians of culture and as a collective are responsible for the behaviours of men and society through parenting, boundaries, influence, sex and relationships."

Eve, the first woman, used her influence to cause Adam to disobey God's instruction, which affected all of mankind. Queen Esther influenced the most powerful man of her time, who ruled an empire of 127 countries. More recently in history, Cleopatra is well known for using her influence over Roman leaders, Julius Caesar and Mark Antony, averting Caesar's plans to capture Egypt to instead serve Egypt. She then consequently became a leader in Egypt.

Esther was merely an orphan, a foreigner and from a tribe of foreigners. Despite this, she was able to influence the king to reverse genocide of the

Jews. Furthermore, she not only overturned the death sentence on her uncle Mordecai, but went on to secure a high-ranking position for him in the palace to replace the king's most respected and senior staff, Haman. As if that was not enough, Esther's influence resulted in justice and Haman's death.

How was a woman from such an obscure and insignificant background able to influence the most powerful man of her day and affect the trajectory of her family, tribe, and whole nation? The answer lies in her feminine superpower, her ability to influence kings.

Like Esther, you can use your influence to save a whole nation, implement justice, avert death and leave a legacy. Woman of God, no matter how obscure or insignificant you may seem today, the trajectory of a person, people, nation, kings, and even a whole generation can be directed by your influence. I implore you to **unlock your influence**!

Let's look at the steps Esther took to overcome her past and move from humble beginnings to the highest seat of influence in her day.

1. Preparation

Esther dedicated 12 months, focused on preparing, upgrading, and learning skills required for her position as the wife of a king. This preparation time was intentional. She dedicated time to heal and upgrade her mindset from that of an orphan and a slave to a queen.

She also took beauty sessions, and most likely etiquette lessons, master classes, courses, and read some books about palace protocol and how to approach, impress, and influence the king. Through preparation and with special favour from God, her coach, and other women, she was promoted to the position of queen and her influence ultimately increased.

2. Coaching

We are told that Esther did everything the Hegai, the king's coach for women, asked her to do. This was the same for Ruth in the Bible when she married Boaz. Naomi coached Ruth on what to do and how to gain Boaz's attention for marriage. Ruth followed her advice and landed a very high-quality man because of her obedience.[9]

Both Hegai and Naomi knew what it took to gain the king's attention and make the women ready for marriage. Hegai and Naomi represents our internal guidance and intuition given by God's Holy Spirit. They also represent coaches, mentors, and advisers who specialise in connecting couples, and getting ladies ready for their purpose husband. I cannot stress enough the importance of both physical and spiritual counselling, coaching or mentorship in your journey to and through marriage. This need for coaching certainly doesn't stop when you get married. In fact, I personally recommend that every couple have a marriage counsellor before and after marriage, especially for couples who grew up in dysfunctional families.

You truly need God's guidance in your everyday life to maintain and grow in attraction with your spouse. You also need good counsel from trained or gifted coaches and experts. Join the Proverbs 31 coaching community where we go through a thorough programme preparing women spiritually, mentally, physically and generationally, to attract, keep and positively influence their purpose partners and marriages.

3.   Honour

Esther needed the king to overturn the death sentence over her race. In putting the request forward, we are told that Esther prepared a banquet for the king. In that banquet, she most likely set up a romantic ambience, prepared the king's favourite meal, had a little dance with her husband, praised and thanked him for how wonderful he was, before delivering her request in a soft, sensual tone while looking and smelling irresistible.

After Esther honoured the king, even before voicing her request, the king was so impressed that he offered to do anything for her up to half of his kingdom. Hint hint, ladies, there is way you can honour your man, and trigger his emotions so much that he meets your needs, and lavishes you with gifts even before you ask!

---

[9] Bible, Ruth 3:4-5

Unlike her predecessor, Vashti, who lost her crown as queen, Esther positioned herself in her femininity, meaning she was not overpowering, disrespectful, forceful, quarrelsome, or emasculating. How many of you have lost the favour of quality men in your lives because of dishonour like Vashti did. Daughter of the king, you must learn the art of influence and dealing with a man's ego through honour and femininity.

4.   Favour

We are told that Esther found favour with the king, his chief coach, Hegai, and everyone who saw her. Favour means preferential treatment beyond what is required. This type of favour comes from a variety of factors including beauty, attraction, charm, character, and spiritual anointing, but, ultimately, is a gift from God.

While Esther found favour with the king, I believe it was equally or even more important that she secured her coach, Hegai's favour as he was the one who prepared and chose the women who went before the king. Hegai most likely would have given her special treatment, shared tips or put in a positive recommendation with the king for Esther, compared to what he did for the other women.

An important secret to learn here about influence is that though we may not always have direct access to or influence over a person, we can influence them indirectly by influencing people who are influential to them. It is also important to note that the biggest influencer on a man's heart is God. Scripture says the heart of a king is in the hand of God, He causes it to go where He chooses.[10]

5.   Spiritual warfare

Despite her ranking as queen in the land, Esther was wise and humble enough to know that her position as queen and her beauty alone, were not enough for a specific request she brought before her husband to reverse the death sentence on the Jews. A legal mandate was already in place, and she knew that a change of law would require divine intervention. In fact, she was very hesitant to put the request to the king, as this was a breach of royal protocol

---

[10] Bible, Proverbs 21:1

and could cost her life and position as queen. She needed God's intervention, and so invoked it through corporate prayers and fasting.

Ladies, we are in the day and age that our beauty, femininity, and sexuality are very important. However, they are not enough all the time, and as women, we need to know how to influence our world through influencing the spiritual realm. We need to regularly humble ourselves and acknowledge our need for God through Prayers. A friend of mine always said "the spiritual controls the physical," meaning that many things that happen in our physical world originate from the spiritual realm. A scripture that worked miracles for me personally in the area of influence is the one that says, "we wrestle not against flesh and blood but spiritual forces."[11] In other words, a wise woman knows when to stop trying to influence the behaviour of people by arguing, fighting, fussing, or nagging. Instead, she must learn to take the fight to the spiritual world through prayers and fasting.

Prayer can change things in the spirit realm, which inevitably manifests physically. The moment we learn to tackle issues on our knees, and subsequently take wise action after praying, is when we will begin to struggle less and save ourselves from frustrations that come with dealing with a man's ego or trying to get men to do things they don't want to do.

The people who know how to influence things spiritually, whether positively or negatively, are the people with the most influence in this world.

---

[11] Bible, Ephesians 6:11

Scripture Recitations

And nations shall come to your light, and kings to the brightness of your rising.

ISAIAH 60:3

The heart of a king is in God's hands and like a river He causes it to go wherever He wills.

PROVERBS 21:3

When the ears heard me, it blessed me and when the eye saw me it gave witness to me.

JOB 29:11

Men listened to me and waited and kept silence for my counsel. After I spoke, they did not speak again, and my word dropped upon them.

JOB 29:21

Prayers

1. Lord, uncover my influence and enlarge my territory, impact, and influence for good.

2. Align my values, mindset and opinions to Your will, wisdom, understanding, purpose, and mission so that I can influence my family for good and not evil, for profit and not for loss, for purpose and not for selfish gains.

3. Lord, bless me with the right words, wisdom, insight, and understanding for positive influence.

4. Promote me to the position of better influence in line with love, light, wisdom, truth, solutions, growth, development, healing, and salvation for myself, my husband, my family, and my world.

5. Position me for greater influence through wisdom, training, favour, promotion, and connections.

6. Let my light shine, and may I no longer be hidden.

7. May my character, love, actions, words, ideas, suggestions, solutions, counsel, and influence affect my husband, friends, family, colleagues, and church positively and purposefully.

8. May my character, love, actions, words, ideas, suggestions, solutions, recommendations, products and services prevail, and influence my world for Your glory.

9. I influence culture and nations around the world for good, in line with Your will and purpose.

10. I will no longer be silenced, ignored, dishonoured, shut down, overlooked, marginalised or bullied.

11. Help me develop a closer relationship with Your Holy Spirit so that I can hear clearly and obey Your guidance for a healthy friendship and relationship with my king.

12. Grant me favour, and connect me with the right people, influencers, coaches, mentors, courses and advisers aligned to my femininity, purpose, mission and influence—people who will connect and prepare me for my king and purpose before and during marriage.

13. I receive Your wisdom and grace on how and when to honour my husband, children, friends, family, and colleagues.

14. I say the right words in the right tone, at the right time and know when to keep quiet.

15. I realise that no matter my status in this world, You are the master influencer so I submit to You through worship, prayer and fasting.

16. I realise that I can influence and cause change, both in the spiritual and physical realm through Prayers, so I have an effective and prevailing prayer life and a better relationship with the Almighty God.

17. I apply self-control, patience, and love so that I do not impose, control, or manipulate but rather influence and inspire while respecting people's rights to choose.

18. Help me to trust You, love people, and not be offended, irrespective of people's choices.

Day 6

AMPLIFY ATTRACTION

The king loved Esther more than all the women in the harem. She found favour and kindness with him more than all the virgins, so that he set the royal crown on her head and made her queen instead of Vashti.

Esther 2:14

In modern society, there are many beautiful women available to a quality man. What then makes a woman stand out so that he chooses her out of the many ladies available to him?

After the honeymoon, what keeps passion alive in your relationship so that your marriage doesn't turn into a dull partnership of two 50 50 roommates?

Attraction is an elixir of your appearance, beauty, character, energy, presence, and spirit, all in one, to make you irresistible and magnetic to the beholder. It is what makes a man notice, find, identify, besotted, pursue, and choose you to be his wife, from many suitors. Attraction is also what causes you and your partner to continue to favour, please, and desire one another after marriage. It helps keep the marriage passionate by making it easier for you and your spouse to show affection and submission to one another and have good sexual chemistry throughout your marriage. Furthermore, when you are attractive, a man automatically and effortlessly assumes the masculine role and wants to pursue, protect, please, and provide for you.

Every woman who desires a passionate marriage MUST put in effort before and during a relationship to ensure that she is attractive externally and internally—in spirit, soul, and body.

Lack of attraction and chemistry has been one of the leading causes of singleness, and marriage breakdown. Many women complain that, after marriage, the man becomes complacent. In some cases, he is unrecognisable and begins to treat her badly. Similarly, a lot of men say that as soon as his wife starts having babies, she lets herself go, and no longer makes efforts to stay attractive. A common reason why a husband's attitude deteriorates after the initial pursuit is because attraction decreases. Efforts around attraction and favour must therefore be taken seriously by both married and unmarried women. If you are single, there is no better time like now to learn about raising your attraction to attract and keep your purpose partner. In my course, I teach about the A, B, C's of attraction—appearance, beliefs, communication and connection, divine favour, emotions, and femininity. I offer tailored advice and support to your specific situation. In this book, because of space limitations, I will cover some of the key points briefly.

Appearance, Beauty Treatments, and Self-care

Queen Esther had a beautiful figure and was lovely to look at. She also spent 12 months getting beauty treatments in preparation for meeting the king.[12] Beauty and image must not be undermined in your quest to be attractive to your king. While character is important, men are visual creatures and are regularly blinded by a woman's beauty. Many high-value, even Christian men go on to marry narcissists and women with poor character because they were blinded by her beauty. This is the power of beauty.

So, while you must work on your character, your character may go unnoticed if there is no external beauty or attraction. We are all beautiful, but like Esther, you must know it and accentuate your beauty through proper self-care, beauty treatments, clothing and a healthy diet. Furthermore, our world is getting more digital, so you need to be intentional about your online appearance and brand.

---

[12] Bible, Esther 2:7

Inner beauty

A huge part of beauty and attraction is internal—psychological and spiritual.

One of Esther's treatments was myrrh, which is an antiseptic, healing and antibacterial treatment. A huge part of a woman's inner beauty treatment to enable her to attract and keep a quality man involves healing and detoxification. How many of us have heard of beautiful and "good character" women who get maltreated or even rejected by men? Tamar in the Bible was such. She was beautiful and well-behaved, however remained desolate, unwanted, and unmarried for the rest of her life. A traumatic event occurred which defiled her spiritually, energetically, emotionally and mentally, rendering her unattractive and unwanted by men.[13]

Actively healing from past trauma and elevating your thought patterns, belief systems, and feelings, impacts on the energy, presence and aura you carry, and inevitably affects your attraction levels. Many women are attractive externally but experience a lot of rejection from men because of their emotional aura which needs to be healed.

We discuss more about healing in the healing chapter in this book. Other aspects of inner beauty, character and femininity, is discussed in upcoming chapters of this book.

Divine Favour

Esther found favour with the king and everyone who saw her. This is important because it is very possible for a woman to be beautiful in every way but not be noticed or favoured by a man enough for him to pursue her to marriage and beyond.

God's gift of favour on a person's life increases their attraction so that a person's internal and external beauty becomes uncovered and highlighted in the beholder's eyes. We must therefore regularly pray to grow in favour with God and men, just as Jesus did.[14]

Let us pray:

---

13 Bible, 2 Samuel 13
14 Bible, Luke 2:52

Scripture Recitation

You are altogether beautiful, my love; there is no flaw in you.

SOLOMON 4:7

And the king will desire your beauty. Since he is your lord, bow to him.

PSALM 45:11

How beautiful you are, my darling, how beautiful you are! Your eyes are like doves. How handsome you are, my beloved, and so pleasant! Indeed, our couch is luxuriant.

SOLOMON 1:15-16

Behold, you are beautiful, my love! Your eyes are doves behind your veil. Your hair is like a flock of goats leaping down the slopes of Gilead. Your teeth are like a flock of shorn ewes that have come up from the washing, all of which bear twins, and not one among them has lost its young. Your lips are like a scarlet thread, and your mouth is lovely. Your cheeks are like halves of a pomegranate behind your veil. Your neck is like the tower of David, built in rows of stone; on it hang a thousand shields, all of them shields of warriors. Your two breasts are like two fawns, twins of a gazelle, that graze among the lilies.

SOLOMON 4:1-16

How beautiful and how delightful you are, My love, with all your charms!

SOLOMON 7:6

Let me hear your voice; For your voice is sweet, And your form is lovely.
SOLOMON 2:14

Scripture Recitation

You have made my heart beat faster, my bride; You have made my heart beat faster with a single glance of your eyes, With a single strand of your necklace. How beautiful is your love, my sister, my bride! How much better is your love than wine, And the fragrance of your oils Than all kinds of spices!

SOLOMON 4:9-10

Prayers

1. Lord, may I grow in favour with God and man.

2. I am a wife who brings favour to my husband and everyone who comes my way.

3. I am a magnet that attracts favour to my life and his.

4. I am irresistibly beautiful and attractive to myself and my king in every way, externally, internally, and with my character.

5. I am physically, emotionally, and spiritually attractive to myself, my husband and my world. He will continually pursue, love, and cherish me.

6. Let my inner beauty—my personality, humour, quirks, wisdom, words, and my quiet, gentle, and peaceful character radiate and captivate his heart.

7. Lord, take off old garments of rejection, dishonour, and shame that hide my attractiveness and cause people to reject or mistreat me.

8. Heal me, deliver and cleanse me from bad spiritual odour, energy, and aura.

9. Heal me from any deep-rooted issues, low self-esteem and fear that act as a repellant to good men and good people.

10. Lord, like Esther, I receive your wisdom on what spiritual and physical diets oils, spices, fragrances, beauty treatments, and content to indulge in order to enhance my beauty and favour.

11. May I never be lazy and let go of my appearance.

12. May my style, clothing, and brand be more and more attractive and alluring daily

13. May I continually be filled with admiration and respect for my husband.

14. Lord, anoint me with oil, anointed words, character and presence that makes me better, most attractive, and most favoured.

15. I become more and more attractive spiritually, mentally and physically as the day goes by.

16. My husband's heart is captivated by all of me: my presence, eyes, smile, body, shape, style, feet, lips, sense of humour, character, kindness and quirks.

17. He is eager to see me and hesitant to leave me always

18. Our bond and attraction for each other spiritually, emotionally, sexually, physically, conversationally, and mentally is magnetic and unbreakable.

.

Day 7

SOUL DETOX AND HEALING

For I will restore health to you And I will heal your wounds,' says the LORD, 'Because they have called you an outcast, saying: "This is Zion; no one seeks her and no one cares for her.

Jeremiah 30:17

One of the biggest reasons many women struggle to attract quality love, and exhibit good feminine character, even when they try, is because of emotional and spiritual wounds.

Despite all your efforts to change, if you are not healed, you will struggle with relationships, be argumentative, stubborn, and find it difficult to operate in your feminine, soft, receptive, trusting, open, and attractive essence. Instead, you will be overly masculine, stubborn, suspicious, untrusting, controlling, competitive, over- giving, and repulsive.

Healing is a way of tackling the roots and seeds that give rise to poor character and outcomes that hinder you from manifesting your purpose marriage. Healing helps you overcome past and childhood trauma, cycles of rejection and neglect, while helping you make positive changes in your life, including improving relationships with your spouse, family, friends, and colleagues, and breaking negative relationships and life cycles. As you heal, you naturally fall into your feminine and become more attractive to your husband, family, and the world around you. People will begin to respond better to you, and you will also attract higher- quality people into your life.

Lessons around healing can be taken from a story in the Bible that describes a farmer who planted seeds on four types of ground. Only one out of four of the grounds yielded a return on his farming investment.

Just like the farmer who planted the seeds on the three different grounds that yielded no return, you may have put in good effort for change, you've done the work—coaching, Prayers, fasting, dating, Bible recitation, generosity, and more. However, all your efforts seem to be in vain and not result in your intended outcomes for a change in character or a healthy relationship and family.

When the farmer planted on "good ground," he yielded a big harvest. This productive ground correlates to a healed heart.

The key to turning your life around, improving character, relationships, being more attractive, manifesting an awesome marriage, breaking negative cycles, and resetting generational legacy is **healing**. Every effort to grow, change, and receive all the good things that God has for you will remain futile if old hurts, rejection, childhood traumas, mother/father wounds, bitterness, divorce, infidelity, pain, and rejection, are not dealt with. Like I explained in the beginning of this book, the Israelites did not enter the land that God promised them, not because Moses was a false prophet who lied about God's will for them to enter their promised land, but because they did not heal from the generational trauma caused from 400 years of slavery.

Today's chapter will be focused on healing the ground of your heart, so that you can manifest a marriage of passion and purpose, and ultimately leave a good legacy for your children.

Three methods for healing can be taken from the parable.

1.   Softening

The first two grounds in the story were stony, with no soil. It was too hard a ground for a seed to be planted or take root. This is comparable to a heart that is so damaged that it has become unresponsive and hard. A person with a hardened heart has lost their ability to love, attach or respond to love. This person is a master at sabotaging love. They are so stubborn, set in their ways, over- defensive, argumentative, and bitter. They cannot see anything wrong with themselves to make a change. It is always another person's fault.

Truths around healing through sermons, teaching, courses, videos, audio, or books—particularly if they are focused on relevant pain points and issues affecting you—are very good ways through which you can heal and soften your heart. From personal experience, my relationship with God through the Bible has kept me sane through very rough times and helped me heal from some trauma. The Bible is God's word, so it carries special power for healing and recreating. God's word is truly like a hammer that breaks the rock into pieces.[15]

Meditation is also a widely attested activity that activates healing. I encourage you to incorporate meditation and solitude into your daily life. Thinking on, imagining, focusing, and repeating specific words, images, sermons, courses, and prayers are all forms of meditation.

2.   Detox and uproot the weeds of bitterness and unforgiveness

Even when a soil is great and healthy, weeds prevent growth by stealing nutrients away from the seed planted, thus suffocating it of nutrients it needs.

Bitterness, which is unresolved hurt and offense that lingers long after an event has happened, is like weeds, and suffocates people, families, relationships, churches, and even our physical body. You may have forgotten a specific event but if unresolved, it can be written into your subconscious, continually causing a lot of problems in relationships and life until it is addressed. Bitterness opens the door to various types of demons and ailments to enter a situation and destroy lives, bodies, and homes.

In your healing process, it is very important to uproot the weeds of bitterness, painful memories, negativity, low self-esteem, hopelessness, and negative belief systems that have been ingrained in you from past experiences. You can do so through:

- Counselling or coaching, where a trained therapist helps you to identify, process and heal from past scenarios and interactions with people who were a source of hurt and bitterness.

---

[15] Bible, Jeremiah 23:9

- Praying and talking to God about your hurts and pain- During prayers, it is good to specifically ask the Lord to help you identify the root and source of bitterness in your life and to help you take the right action to heal.
- Meditation, by focusing on and visualising new positive images, scenarios, and words related to healing and the new reality you want to experience.

Other effective methods of healing that have positively impacted me include journaling, letter writing, worship, crying, and reciting prophetic or affirmative words.

3.   Faith Food

In farming, the ground is prepared for growth by feeding the soil with water, fertiliser, and nutrients it needs. Likewise, it is important that you inject positive food and nutrients into your heart for healing. We already spoke about the power of God's word and meditation for healing. Some other nutrients necessary to feed, heal and soften the ground of your heart are words of affirmation, prophecies, personal development, coaching, courses, and love.

4.   Love

Love is one of the most powerful nutrients for healing your heart, and the most powerful source of love is God. God is love. His love is most felt when you get to know Him. Other powerful sources of love are self-love and from people who are loving towards you. It is my prayer for you and your family, that you will become acquainted with God's love and that you will love yourself and encounter people who will practically love you in areas that you need to be loved and healed. Gary Chapman describes practical ways and languages in which we receive and give love including quality time, affirmation, giving, service and touch. He goes on to state that we all have primary ways in which we understand love. For example, some people feel most loved through quality time, others it feel most loved by receiving gifts.

I pray for you that you will be loved practically in the language that your soul understands.

I also pray that God will remove you from environments and people who deplete your love tank through rejection, neglect, jealousy, unsupportiveness and hatred.

Let us pray:

Scripture Recitation

Search me, God, and know my heart; test me and know my anxious thoughts. See if there is any offensive way in me and lead me in the way everlasting.

PSALM 139:24

Look after each other so that none of you fails to receive the grace of God. Watch out that no poisonous root of bitterness grows up to trouble you, corrupting many.

HEBREW 12:15

And I will give you a new heart, and I will put a new spirit in you. I will take out your stony, stubborn heart of stone and give you a tender, responsive heart of flesh.

EZEKIEL 36:26

He said, "If you will listen carefully to the voice of the LORD your God and do what is right in his sight, obeying his commands and keeping all his decrees, then I will not make you suffer any of the diseases I sent on the Egyptians; for I am the LORD who heals you.

EXODUS 15:26

Scripture Recitation

Do not conform to this world but let God transform you into a new person by changing the way you think. Then you will learn to know God's will for you, which is good and pleasing and perfect.

ROMANS 12:2

Finally, brothers, whatever is true, whatever is honorable, whatever is just, whatever is pure, whatever is lovely, whatever is commendable, if there is any excellence, if there is anything worthy of praise, think about these things.

PHILLIPIANS 4:8

Your unfailing love, O LORD, is as vast as the heavens; your faithfulness reaches beyond the clouds. Your righteousness is like the mighty mountains, Your justice like the ocean depths. You care for people and animals alike, O LORD. How precious is Your unfailing love, O God! All humanity finds shelter in the shadow of Your wings

PSALM 36:5-7

And may you have the power to understand, as all God's people should, how wide, how long, how high, and how deep his love is. May you experience the love of Christ, though it is too great to understand fully. Then you will be made complete with all the fullness of life and power that comes from God.

EPHESIANS 3:18

But God showed His great love for us by sending Christ to die for us while we were still sinners. (Romans 5:8)

ROMANS 5:8

Prayers

1. Thank you, Lord, that You are a God who cares about my wellbeing and you heal my broken-heart.

2. You are my source of healing, and I come to You as my healer.

3. Search me, oh Lord, and heal me of any incidents, thoughts, or memories from my childhood, past relationships, feuds, betrayals, current relationships, and life events that negatively affect my life, marriage, and relationships.

4. Soften and heal my heart with Your word and Your love.

5. Deliver me from hardness and stubbornness of heart that cause me to sabotage relationships and give me a tender heart responsive to love.

6. Send Your word and heal me, convict, and change my heart and deliver me from all destructive thinking patterns, beliefs, and ways.

7. I uproot and let go of bitterness, hurt, pain, rejection, disappointments, betrayals from my heart.

8. I choose and receive forgiveness, love, healing, peace, and deliverance for my soul.

9. Lord, heal me, and deliver me from the effects of rejection, disappointment, criticism, abuse, negative words, and curses from all my past relationships with parents, siblings, friends and loved ones, ex-boyfriends or husband, colleagues, church members, or even fore parents.

10. I am healed from all strongholds, including habitual sins, low self-esteem, moodiness, rudeness, pride, impatience, negative thinking, anger, laziness, and sluggishness.

11. I am healed from father or mother wounds of rejection, neglect, abuse, criticism, accusation and betrayals.

12. The seed of love, healing, forgiveness, many good experiences and memories, are planted into my subconscious, conscious mind, and reality.

13. Help my disbelief and all areas of doubt, cynicism, and hopelessness because of past hurt and experiences.

14. Help me renew and upgrade my mind and way of thinking so that I can be transformed to the best and most attractive version of me.

15. Cleanse my mind, conscience, subconscious and conscious mind, and memories with the blood of Jesus.

16. I receive Your love, and I am forgiven.

17. Open my eyes and my heart to know and realise God's love and forgiveness for me. Help my doubts and false beliefs about Your love for me.

18. I encounter people who actively demonstrate God's love for me and speak my love languages, including practical service, generosity, gifts, encouragement, appreciative words, active listening, quality time, and more.

19. Similarly, I am a conduit of God's love to my spouse, children, family, friends, clients, strangers, and colleagues.

Day 8

FEMININE COMMUNICATION

She opens her mouth with wisdom, and the teaching of kindness is on her tongue.

-Proverbs 31:26

The words we speak are one of the most powerful tools we have as humans. In fact, a woman's words are a secret weapon for influencing situations, both in the spiritual and physical realms, with your spouse, children, and people within your sphere of influence. A woman's words of affirmation, encouragement, praise, suggestions, and ideas can turn a very ordinary man into a superhero. Likewise, your tongue can tear and shut a man right down and destroy your relationships. Unfortunately, many women are either not aware of this or have used their tongues to tear down their homes, hinder their man's dreams, and caused problems in their relationships. Many women, through gossip, have damaged relationships and reputations.

Unfortunately, in some cultures, it is very common for mothers to curse their children when they are upset. Strong curses such as "it will not be well with you," "you will amount to nothing," "you're a problem child," "problems will always come your way" are spewed out so easily. I have witnessed and heard of many situations where the child who got so much cursing from their mother ended up manifesting exactly what the mother said.

Whether you use deep curses or any form of negative words or cussing with your spouse and children, these can have very detrimental effects on their lives, your relationships, and home. It is, therefore, very important that you work on and pray about the words that come out of your mouth. As scripture says: "The wise woman builds her house, but, with her own hands, the foolish one tears it down."[16]

The Proverbs 31 woman spoke in wisdom and kindness. This means that she knew what to say, when to say it, and when not to say anything at all. Her words carried value and brought solutions to the problems she, her children, family members, colleagues, and clients faced. She was full of wise counsel, problem-solving ideas, and creativity. Who knows, perhaps people paid her for her advice and counsel.

A woman with "the teaching of kindness is in her tongue" knows how to teach, correct, influence, and set boundaries with tact and kindness. Scriptures say, "a soft answer turns away wrath."[17] This type of woman knows how to give kind responses during hostile situations and to sooth a troubled soul. Daughter of the king, wouldn't you want to be like her?!

In dating and relationships women struggle like I did in their communication with men. Many women in my practice complain about their encounters with men as being very boring, mundane and challenging. With wisdom and tact, however, women can learn to turn mundane or challenging situations with men around, resolve conflict, set boundaries and learn how to spark attraction, inspire pursuit, masculinity and commitment in her relationship through feminine communication. The same principles apply and can be used outside of romantic relationships, at work and in business.

To be like the Proverbs 31 woman, and build trust and emotional connection with a man, you will need to

1.   Have a whole and healed heart

Pray healing Prayers, see a therapist and take actions around healing the heart and forgiving past hurts. From the abundance of the heart, the mouth speaks.[18] Irrespective of how much you try, if your heart is not healed, hurtful

---

[16] 16 Bible, Proverbs 14:1
[17] 17 Bible, Proverbs 15:1
[18] Bible, Matthew 12:34

things will come out of your mouth, especially during stressful situations. As the saying goes: hurt people hurt people.

2.　　Retrain yourself to communicate from your feminine state

This is important especially when setting boundaries, correcting a man, resolving conflict or inspiring him to meet your needs. As described in an earlier chapter, your feminine state is a state of being where you are rested, trusting, open, vulnerable, flexible, agreeable, pleasant, and playful, rather than struggling, hustling, controlling, pursuing, competitive or argumentative. When communicating from your feminine you communicate with gratitude, gentleness, humility, love, understanding, flexibility, vulnerability, and expressing how you feel, as opposed to communicating rudely, with arrogance, stubbornness and judgment. For examples:

'I really love it how you open doors for me and pull out my chair when we go out. It makes me feel cherished, safe and cared for'.

'I love how you spend quality time with the children. It makes me feel so grateful and blessed to have a husband and baby father like you. You're the best honestly!'.

You can also successfully resolve conflict and influence a man to meet your needs without fighting or fussing, through feminine communication. I first learned the boundary sandwich method for influencing men to listen and meet your needs from my mentor Chengi Tobun.

For example when you want him to do house chores you can say

'You are such a good man and I really love how you serve people and do a lot for this family. I am just feeling exhausted and unsupported with the house chores especially when the trash is not being taken out. How can we fix this?

Or when you want him to spend more quality time with you

'Hunni when is a good time to talk?.....

'I would love it if we spent more quality time together. When you are too busy, or on your phone while on our date, it doesn't make me feel good, I would prefer it if we spend more undistracted time together. What do you think?'

In my coaching practice, I go in-depth into feminine communication where we cover topics such as how to build emotional connection, attraction and commitment with your man, and resolve conflict in a way that inspires your man to meet your needs. I offer scripts, training and coaching for common and specific scenarios you will encounter in dating, marriage and day to day relationships..

3.   Affirm, appreciate and admire your man

Most importantly a feminine woman must always affirm, appreciate and praise her man at every chance she gets, even when she is correcting him. This brings the king out of him and is a secret to influencing him to be a better man and to love and meet your needs better. Whether married or not, you must begin to put this principle into practice with the men in your life, and with friends and family.

I pray for you, precious daughter of the Highest, that you will always use your words positively to influence, build up, heal, encourage, counsel, teach, and add value. You will quickly solve problems, resolve conflict and there will be gold in your tongue. You will also exercise self-control so that you don't use words that tear down, kill, and destroy; you will ever encourage even when annoyed.

Let us pray:

Scripture Recitation

Let the words of my mouth and the meditation of my heart be acceptable in Your sight, O Lord, my rock and my redeemer.

PSALM 19:13-14

Set a guard, O Lord, over my mouth; keep watch over the door of my lips! Do not let my heart incline to any evil.

PSALM 141:3-4

Let no corrupting talk come out of your mouths, but only such as is good for building up, as fits the occasion, that it may give grace to those who hear.

EPHESIANS 4:29

And by their word every dispute and every assault shall be settled.

DEUTERONOMY 21:15

Gracious words are like a honeycomb, sweetness to the soul and health to the body.

PROVERBS 16:24

Let your conversation be always full of grace, seasoned with salt, so that you may know how to answer everyone.

COLOSSIANS 4:6

The Sovereign LORD has given me his words of wisdom, so that I know how to comfort the weary. Morning by morning he wakens me and opens my understanding to his will.

ISIAIAH 50:4

Prayers

1. Let the words of my mouth and meditation of my heart be acceptable in Your sight, oh Lord.

2. Heal and cleanse my heart and thought processes so that I speak only what is good, kind, wholesome, wise, soothing to the soul, and uplifting to people's spirit.

3. I choose to dwell and think about whatever is pure, positive, soothing, encouraging, praiseworthy, kind, and true.

4. I receive wisdom to speak the right words at the right time that will encourage, build up, and heal the hearers, including my husband, children, and family.

5. My wise words will lead to passion, purpose, and profit; love and blessed generational legacy.

6. My words, tone and voice are like honey to my husband, soothing, calming, and nourishing to his soul and spirit, and health to his body.

7. Holy Spirit power and anointing is in my tongue. Depression, anxiety, and confusion flee when I speak.

8. I receive and apply wisdom with my words to solve problems, resolve conflict, speak the truth, be transparent and correct in love.

9. I receive the spirit of self-control to speak the right words at the right time always, and to know when to be quiet, irrespective of how upset I feel.

10. I will not speak hurtful or discouraging words. Rather, I will know when to be silent and pray.

11. I am slow to speak, slow to anger, but quick to listen with empathy and understanding.

12. I open my tongue with wisdom, and the law of kindness is in my tongue.

13. My family eat the good of my words all the days of their lives.

14. There is gold in my tongue. My words carry value, healing, counsel, influence, solutions, and treasures.

15. Let the words I write and speak turn away wrath and anger and replace it with life, peace, and transformation.

16. My words resolve problems, sets boundaries, cast out demons, and bring peace, profit and reconciliation to chaos in homes, families, relationships, and friendships.

17. Death and life are in the power of my tongue. I exercise the power and authority of my words to heal, quicken, and bring life to dead and hopeless situations.

18. Like Jesus and his disciples, demons and negative spirits flee at the sound of my voice and my written words, in Jesus' name.

Day 9

TIME MANAGEMENT

Pay careful attention, then, to how you walk, not as unwise but as wise, making the best use of the time, because the days are evil.

-Ephesians 5:15-16

The Proverbs 31 woman was a wife and a mother who had her family, home, businesses, properties, and staff, all demanding her time and attention. She was just like the modern woman, who must balance the demands of being a wife, mother, homemaker, business(es) owner, influencer, and friend, all at once.

To achieve all that she did and be the role model that she is for wives today, the Proverbs 31 woman had excellent time management skills, such as discipline, efficiency, and the wisdom on how and when to prioritise the different demands on her time. Being able to work smart and not necessarily hard was key, which means she knew when to do things herself, and when to delegate or employ help. Only a few of us get this right.

Understandably, it is not uncommon for wives to struggle to keep the balance. Many try so hard to meet the demands on their lives by themselves while neglecting themselves, their wellbeing, appearance, friendships or even their family. They are stressed and become unhealthy and out of shape as a result. Some end up with severe illnesses due to stress.

It is worth reiterating that the Proverbs 31 woman had maids. Delegation and employing help to achieve tasks at home or in business is a no-brainer for efficient and wise feminine wives.

To improve your time management, tackle these common factors that affect time-management:

1. Focus
2. Planning and prioritising
3. Distractions
4. Delay
5. Sluggishness

These must be eliminated to allow for better time management.

Distractions and delays

One of the biggest stealers of purpose, time, and destiny are distractions and delays. Distractions are the most commonly used spiritual arrows used to delay or stop you from fulfilling your purpose by stealing your attention and effort away from what really matters to your success, destiny, and purpose. In today's social media age, we are continuously bombarded with distractions from the internet. Unfortunately, most of us succumb and become slaves to social media. An alarming 210 million people are estimated to be addicted to social media. Several studies into its effect on the brain have shown that internet use changes brain function and has a negative impact on memory and one's ability to concentrate. Aside from social media many things happen to distract our attention.

Sluggishness, discouragement, and delay

Sluggishness is another form of delay to prevent planned activities from occurring at the appointed time. It is anything intrinsic to us or another person that slows our activities down, such as a brain fog, disappointment, discouragement, conflict, and weariness which slow us down from fulfilling purpose and projects on time, or at all.

At the time of writing this book, several disappointing events happened one after the other around the whole process of publishing this book, from poor service to close friends acting strangely, jealousy and poor support from friends with the book, and even several things in my home breaking down all at the same time which took my attention! It was so obvious, with the barrage of events, that I was under spiritual attack because of the book. I literally gave up. My coach and one or two friends encouraged me to push through, knowing that the numerous distractions were an indication that a great thing, greater than I imagined, was about to be birthed with this book. However, I still struggled for months alone to finish off the book. I started to talk myself out of my goals for the book. Soon after giving up, Bishop Tuffour who knew nothing about my book or what I was going through at the time, gave me a prophetic message in line with my original goals for the book and more. This prophetic word gave me the strength and renewed hope to finish the last lap of the book.

Eliminating delays and distractions

Discipline, focus, and concentration help you overcome distractions and must be intentionally exercised. For example, go on regular internet fasts, shutting down your phone regularly while you meditate or read.

To overcome distraction, you must master focus. Take time to do an audit. What activities must be prioritized to allow you achieve your goals, purpose, and God's instructions for your life at this time? Be aware of the distractions sent to slow you down and shift your focus on the task ahead. What activities are taking up your time that must be eliminated to allow you focus on your priorities, purpose, and success?

At the time of publishing this book the Lord led me to give up secular work, time with some friends and several volunteering activities I was involved with. It was very hard to say no to people I love. Some people were offended but it was clear that my purpose of writing this book, supporting women through the P31 community, improving my femininity, and getting myself and others ready to meet our husbands required me to let go of the busy life and to be more focused.

It's worth noting that sometimes, events that are beyond your control can often happen to distract you, such as illness, accidents, quarrels, bereavement, loss, or IT/technical challenges. If this is the case, be aware of why the barrage of distractions is happening—that is to distract you from purpose—and commit it to the Lord in Prayers.

Planning prayerfully

The single most important factor to help you achieve tasks on time, is planning and praying. Plan and prioritise your activities weekly, monthly, or quarterly, in line with your goals. Eliminate or spend less time and energy on things and people that don't align with your goals. It's also very important to pray for and commit your plans to God daily, while being open to changing your plans as God directs. Ideally, make it a habit to plan the night before for the day ahead, plan at the weekend for the week ahead, and the end of the month for the month ahead.

Miracle mornings

Finally, as a wife (or wife-to-be), it is very important to prioritise your quiet time in meditation, where you shut down all noise and distractions, get quiet and journal, pray, meditate, and engage in fellowships with God and His word.

In his book Miracle Morning, Elrod describes six practices in the morning- which he abbreviates as SAVERS- that will transform you and help you lead a productive life. These are silence (and mediation), affirmations, visualization or imaginations, exercise, reading and scribing.

This book helps you practice four of the miracle morning practices (meditation, affirmation, reading and scribing). Perhaps for the rest of this 31 days challenge or after, gradually incorporate more of the 6 practices each morning, using the affirmations in this book each day.

Included in your resource pack is a habit and time management tracker to help you manage your time and track your progress. Trackers are very helpful for time management and resetting habits. Download your miracle morning and time management tracker from
www.myproverbs31family.com/POP31bonuses

Let us pray:

Scripture Recitation

Look carefully then how you walk, not as unwise but as wise, making the best use of the time, because the days are evil. Therefore, do not be foolish, but understand what the will of the Lord is.

EPHESIANS 5:15-17

So teach us to number our days that we may get a heart of wisdom.

PSALM 90:12

The Spirit of God hath made me, And the breath of the Mighty doth quicken me.

JOB 33:4

Turn away mine eyes from beholding vanity and quicken thou me in thy way.

PSALM 119:37

Share your plans with the LORD, and you will succeed

PROVERBS 16:3

I rise before dawn and cry for help; I have put my hope in your word.

PSALM 119:147

My voice shalt thou hear in the morning, O LORD; in the morning will I direct my prayer unto thee, and will look up.

PSALM 5:3

Prayers

1. Lord, give me wisdom, grace, and power to effectively manage my time.

2. Help me to plan and prioritise daily, weekly, monthly, quarterly, and yearly.

3. Give me wisdom to prioritise appropriately in line with my God-given purpose, family, success, and productivity, knowing what work to do now, delay, delegate or decline.

4. Teach me how to increase my effectiveness and efficiency so I work smarter, effectively, efficiently, proficiently, and profitably.

5. Lord, increase my productivity so that I do more effective work in less time.

6. I achieve purposeful and profitable outcomes; I make a difference, and everything I do succeeds.

7. Send all the right people, staff, business partners, home-workers, cleaners, cooks, contractors, workmen and nannies, to work with me in line with prophesy, purpose, productivity, proficiency, destiny, and correct timing.

8. Remove all distractions, time-wasters, discouragers, disappointments, and enemies of progress away from my sphere of influence.

9. Forgive me, Lord, and deliver me from indiscipline, character flaws, and addictions that slow me down.

10. I recognise and eliminate activities, people, and interests that are a distraction from purpose, productivity and profit.

11. I have a sound mind. I am focused and disciplined.

12. Bless, anoint, quicken, and heal my neurons, brain, and mind.

13. Heal me from phone, social media and internet addictions, chemical imbalances, insomnia, brain fog, and sluggishness in my mind.

14. All parts of my brain and cells responsible for speed, focus, concentration, accuracy, creativity, and activity be quickened and function optimally, in Jesus' name.

15. Let Your Holy Spirit heal and quicken my mind, in Jesus' name. Quicken every sleeping or dormant brain cell that affect performance and creativity.

16. Give me focus, concentration, and speed and help me overcome distractions, lack of focus, and sluggishness.

17. In the name of Jesus, and by the blood of Jesus, the spirit of delay, sluggishness, sabotage, monitoring spirit, and human agents of the enemy, sent to slow me down is rebuked and defeated.

18. I act now and say yes to my priorities. I say no to all distractions, procrastination and addictions, in Jesus' name.

19. I abort demonic distractions, discouragement, and disappointments, people, plans or events and rebuke every spirit or person who has been sent to waste my time or delay my purpose, in the name of Jesus.

20. There will be no holdups, holdouts, setbacks or delays on my projects, purpose, and success, in Jesus' name.[19]

21. I wake up every morning experiencing and practicing miracle mornings, afternoons and evenings

---

[19] Adapted from Cindy Trimm's Entrepreneurship Prayers.

Day 10

FEMININE ENTREPRENEURSHIP

She seeks wool and flax and works with willing hands. She considers a field and buys it; With the fruit of her hands, she plants a vineyard. She sees that her trading is profitable, and her lamp does not go out at night.

-Proverbs 31:13, 16, 18

The Proverbs 31 woman was very creative and productive. She was a successful business owner, grew a garden, and ran various creative and profitable businesses.

Feminine nature is very creative. You will naturally become more creative, productive, and profitable when you tap more into your feminine nature. As you slow down, heal, and let go of emotional baggage, toxicity and hustle, and embrace space, self-care, and self-awareness, your mind is freer and more creative.

As you become more creative and align with your purpose and passions, you will feel a strong sense of intrinsic satisfaction, confidence, joy, and accomplishment. This automatically affects how you show up in the world—with radiance, effervescence, and sparkle. Furthermore, wealth, entrepreneurship, and passive income become natural byproducts of tapping into feminine creativity.

For the single woman desiring marriage, singleness is certainly a very good time for you to access your creativity, align with purpose and build up financial acumen. Moreover, the Bible says that your gifts will bring you before kings, meaning that walking in your gifts, talents, and creativity will automatically raise the calibre of people you meet as friends, colleagues, dating or relationship partners, while reducing your chances of settling into a marriage out of desperation.

For the married woman, tapping into feminine creativity, entrepreneurship, and productivity gives you a sense of worth, radiance, and glow that raises your attraction and gives a positive boost to your marriage.

Here are a few tips I have applied and observed that have connected me to creativity, productivity, and entrepreneurship:

Femininity

As I embarked on my healing and femininity journey, let go of toxicity and decluttered my life and friendships, ideas and content began to flow out of me. As someone who suffered from multiple learning difficulties and had so many challenges around writing and confidence, I never believed in a million years that writing a book was possible for me.

Sitting in your feminine essence of rest, healing, wellbeing, trust, self-love, attraction, and other feminine characteristics discussed earlier, creates an atmosphere that ignites your creativity and ingenuity, which when branded can create an unlimited amount of wealth and products the world can benefit from.

The possibilities are endless when you step into your feminine power. Your mind becomes decluttered of all the dirt and hurt clogging it up, and free to accomplish its purpose to create, give birth to, and nurture new ideas and solutions into reality.

Friendships and environment

Assessing the type of friends, family, and church colleagues and leaders I had around me was life changing. Noticing the people in my life who I regarded much higher than they did me, received a lot from me but gave very little, were silent and unsupportive when I needed them, was one of the most painful experiences I went through in my life. However this realisation enabled me to be intentional and make room for the type of mutually beneficial relationships I needed for the next level in my purpose path.

Elevating your friendships and environments from people who look or talk down, compete with and disrespect you, to fellow entrepreneurs or people who will mutually support your business, is key. As I prayed for God to give me mutually beneficial friendships, where the adoration, love, support and respect were mutual, a strange thing happened. I lost even more friends. However, over time this gave me more space in my life to get closer to God, have more time to think and create, and make space for friends who were more aligned to my purpose, creativity, and entrepreneurship. Connecting with my coach and mentors who were already in business, automatically unlocked my own creativity.

Turn your mess into a message; your pain into purpose

Leaning into God during immense pain elevates you spiritually and gives birth to creativity, revelation, and ideas. You discover the deepest truth and lessons in your pain. These lessons can be turned into solutions, transformational steps and processes that can be packaged into a profitable book, course, workshop, coaching programme, or even a charity or movement. It is truly a miracle.

The most painful year of my life—when I literally came to the end of myself—was when I met God in a new way I had never experienced before. Streams of creativity, ideas, blogs, and books flowed freely. Listening and obeying God's still small voice and instructions during my pain, plus His grace and empowerment, gave birth to the Proverbs 31 community.

Letting Go of the 9-5 Slavery system

A big aspect of femininity is slowing down, making space and time for self-care, creativity and passions. One huge way to do that is to let go of your 9-5 job either completely, gradually, or partially by becoming a part time worker. In his book the 4 hours Work Week, Tim Ferriss encouraged his readers to leave the current system which traps most people into a life of spending their youthful years working on a job they probably hate, while postponing freedom and liberty to older years when they are frail. Tim offers an alternative to live this life of freedom now, through business, entrepreneurship and eliminating unfruitful work, while automating or delegating work to create freedom and time for the things you enjoy. I agree with Tim and teach women in my community who want to, to work towards leaving behind the 9-5 system, embracing what I call femininepreneurship by setting up businesses more aligned with their passions, purpose and profit with less stress, less hustle and bustle, and more time for self-care, play, family and rest.

Today, I pray that your creativity, God given gifts and talents, profitable ideas, solutions and strategies currently hidden under the covering of over-masculinity, depression, overworking, low self-esteem, and pain, will be awakened, realised and utilised.

You, yes, you beautiful, are gifted and talented. God needs to make use of your gifts, pain and past experiences to fulfil His purpose. Your husband needs your gifts, talents and experiences. Your children need them. The world needs them. God can turn your pain into purpose and profit for His glory.

The world awaits your manifestation, woman of God. May you no longer be hidden, suppressed, and weighed down by the cares of this life. Rather arise and shine, and begin to manifest your God- given gifts and talents, all for His glory. At the end of the world, when God asks about what you did with His gifts, talents, and femininity, may you yield a good return on God's investment.

Let us pray:

Scripture Recitation

Arise, shine, for your light has come, And the glory of the Lord has risen upon you.

For behold, darkness shall cover the earth, and thick darkness the peoples; But the Lord will arise upon you, And His glory will be seen upon you. Nations shall come to your light, and kings to the brightness of your rising.

ISAIAH 60: 1–3

Instead of shame and dishonor, you will enjoy a double share of honor. You will possess a double portion of prosperity in your land, and everlasting joy will be yours.

ISAIAH 61:7

The LORD will open the heavens, the storehouse of His bounty, to send rain on your land in season and to bless all the work of your hands. You will lend to many nations but will borrow from none.

DEUTERONOMY 28:12

May the favour of the Lord our God rest on us; and make our efforts successful. Yes, make our efforts successful!

PSALM 90:17

The LORD will guarantee a blessing on everything you do and will fill your storehouses with grain. The LORD your God will bless you in the land He is giving you.

DEUTERONOMY 28:12

Prayers

1. Lord, help me to be still and abide in the Lord and thus reap the fruitfulness that comes from solitude, slowing down and listening to God.

2. Awaken my creativity, femininity, and entrepreneurship.

3. Lord, forgive me for burying and not using my God-given gifts, talents, and ideas.

4. Give me the courage and clarity to arise and shine in my light, gifts and talents

5. Turn my pain into purpose, my struggles into strategy, my mess into a message, movement and ministry that is profitable to me and the world at large.

6. Awaken and uncover all sleeping potentials, gifts, and talents, including the ones that I had and lost, those that are not yet realised, and those that I have but not using.

7. Lead me along my purpose path and may I be aligned with, and profitable in purpose.

8. My creative muscles, brain cells, and neurons come to life.

9. All dormant or suppressed gifts, ideas, and inventions come alive now in the name of Jesus.

10. I arise and shine with my gifts, talents, ideas, inventions, and businesses.

11. My profitable business ideas, creative inventions, winning strategies, problem-solving projects, profitable songs, blogs, books, videos, films, courses, schools, ventures, causes, and charities awake, arise,

shine, manifest, and become a reality, in Jesus' name [repeat this 3 times].

12. Holy Spirit, breathe on my struggles, mind, brain, work ideas, inventions, and thoughts, and let them come alive and be turned into successful 6/7/8 figure businesses and projects that are highly profitable.

13. I pray against the following missiles sent to keep me down and ineffective in this world:
    o Sabotage
    o Sluggishness
    o Brain fog
    o Tiredness
    o Distractions
    o Laziness
    o Self-doubt
    o Low self-esteem
    o Dishonour
    o Limiting beliefs
    o Rejection
    o Discouragement
    o Jealousy
    o Frenemies
    o Gossip and slander
    o Fear and anxiety

14. Let everything I put my hands to do be successful.

15. Everything I touch turns to gold.

16. I receive wisdom, ideas, and purposeful connections to be profitable with my work.

17. Grant me the courage to let go of people, things and work that is not aligned with my God given passions, purpose and profit.

18. The works of my hands are blessed. I manifest wisdom, wealth, and profit with my work.

19. My gifts create opportunities for me and connect me with kings, queens, and purpose people.

20. I am diligent, disciplined, and honourable and excellent in all I do.

21. Open the heaven and storehouse of blessing, favour, and wisdom on my business. May I yield a large harvest in all my endeavours

Day 11

MAKE HOME A HEAVENLY HAVEN

A wise woman builds her home, but a foolish woman tears it down with her own hands.

Proverbs 14:1

Within every woman lies the power and authority to either build or destroy her home. You have the power to direct the affairs of your home and its residents in the direction that you desire, for better or for worse. Women are also the gatekeepers of their homes. This means that you have the power to allow or disallow spirits, energy, or ambience into your home, and drive out ailments and negativity from your home. Unfortunately, many women are either unaware of their superpowers or use it wrongly.

The home environment affects all areas of life, including mental health, career, destiny, and relationships. The home environment has the power to make or break you, propel you into purpose, set you back by years and decades, or even destroy your future. Furthermore, the home environment a person grows up in sets the trajectory for their future relationships. A toxic and chaotic home environment during childhood is a big reason why many are battling with singleness, divorces and failed relationships.

Every wife must therefore intentionally learn to build her home using the following building blocks:

1.   Peace

As someone who grew up in a very toxic home environment, I cannot emphasise enough the importance and benefits of a peaceful home. People who have one, take it for granted until they taste what it feels like for a day to be in a home where quarrelling, fights, noise, and sleepless nights are the norm.

I learnt my lessons about the importance of a stable home environment and how to implement peace amid chaos through my negative experiences. Quarrelling, fights, betrayals, bitterness, and noise were my reality for a very long time. Though I suffered a great deal as a result, and am still on my healing journey, I can only give God praise and thanks for coming out of my home situation alive and with my mind intact. He really is a God who is with His children as they go through the fire.

As a result of the chaos, I regularly suffered from chronic insomnia. I remember a particular time I was not sleeping at all for days and weeks at a time while I also had very tough exams and was working at the same time. During this time, one of my household members would exercise close to midnight hours in a room that was directly above mine, so I would hear jumping and banging like it was literally inside my head. Once my sleep got interrupted at that time of the night, that would be the end of sleeping for me until the morning when it was time to go to work. Another family member would start cooking at very odd hours of the morning, sometimes 2, 3, or 4 am. As the walls were thin and the kitchen near my bedroom, I would hear the squeaking sounds right in my ear. If hell existed on earth, I swear my home was a living hell and many times I thought I would prefer to die rather than live through the hell I was going through. I often thought about suicide and attempted it one time. Thankfully the Lord saved my life during that suicide ordeal and delivered me completely from suicidal thoughts.

This chaotic home environment affected my performance at work and school, my relationships, and even my faith. I was so unhappy. My confidence was very low and I was in no position to date. Words can't describe the pain I went through. It was truly a miracle I came out of that ordeal without going mad.

The cycle continued night after night and no amount of begging, shouting, yelling, or quarrelling stopped the noise. In fact, the more I would plead, quarrel and ask people to stop exercising and cooking late at night, the worse and more frequent the noise became. Every night was an argument over the same issue. Fights and police calls were a regular occurrence in my household.

One day, I met a lady in church. With tears, I explained what I had been going through at home. She looked at me almost in shock and with her Nigerian accent said, "Is that what you are crying over? Are you not a Christian? Don't you pray? Why can't you drive the demons out of your house?"

I didn't know whether to be upset at this lady that she didn't feel sorry for me, but her words that night changed not only my home life but many areas of my life forever. Since then we became a very good friends. I will never forget her.

I took her advice and began to pray and speak scriptures over my home. God gave me a scripture in Isaiah 32:18, which I would speak repeatedly in prayers.

Like magic, without having to fight and fuss, the late-night exercising and cooking stopped! It was a miracle and happened the first day I started praying over my home. After a long period of stillness, there would be times the noise and fights would start again, but rather than confronting people I would pray scriptures and rebuke demons privately. I basically re-channeled the energy I would use to quarrel, fuss and fight into prayers, reciting scriptures and rebuking demons who were using members of my family to get at me. This may sound irrational, but the fact is, this technique worked wonders for my home life and in fact the quarrelling, screaming, and police calls reduced significantly after this simple act. I have many miracle stories during my time in my family home. One lesson I learnt which I apply to all areas of my life and relationships, is that many times our fights and quarrels with people have a spiritual source. Scriptures emphasise repeatedly that we are not fighting people, but demons. However, most of us, unaware of this principle, expend so much time and energy nagging and quarrelling with people instead of handling matters spiritually through prayers and declarations. As a feminine woman, you must learn how to expel the spirits of confusion and demonic dramas out of our homes, environments, and relationships. Do so using the name, word and blood of Jesus Christ, because in Christ Jesus lies the power to fight and overcome demons.

More practical ideas on how to create peace in your home are discussed below.

2. Set a good ambience and presence in your home

You are the thermostats for your home, and you must be intentional to ensure that the ambience in your home is godly, peaceful, loving, and joyful. Good ambience is important for creating an atmosphere of peace and happiness but also ignites the creativity of all members of a household. It is your role as the feminine to ensure that your husband and children can't wait to come home. Your home must be yours, your man's and children's haven, comfort, and healing zone. Visitors who visit must also notice the peace in your home.

The best and most effective way to do this is through Prayers. You need to make your home a house of prayer and worship. In addition to your private times of prayer, set intentional times aside for family devotion, discussions, and prayers. This could be daily or weekly but should be a time when TV and social media are turned off and all members of the household come together to interact in worship, and conversations. Make time regularly to peacefully resolve conflicts during these family dates. Don't forget to regularly laugh and play together as a family.

3. Keep a clean and organised environment

In addition to setting the spiritual atmosphere through prayers, keeping a tidy and a beautiful home is very important in creating a good ambience in the home. Ideally the whole family should take up the tasks to clean up and decorate, or you can employ help to periodically clean, organise, and decorate your home. The Proverbs 31 woman had maids and staff who helped her at home.

A clean and well-decorated home full of nice smells help in setting a beautiful ambience. If you haven't got into the habit of burning candles, and having candle-lit dinners with your spouse, set yourself a target to do so fortnightly, monthly or quarterly. Essential oils, including myrrh, are also great for good ambience.

4.   Words

The words you speak and the way people speak to one another in your home is very important. I like the saying "only good vibes." In other words, set a boundary that everyone in your home, including visitors, must always be kind and speak words of kindness and encouragement. Once the insults and dishonour start, you must call it out quickly. Teach your children to be kind, listen, and be honouring of one another. Teach them by your examples with them and your spouse. Have conversations about the importance of kindness and honour. You can also display quotes and words that have the principles you want adopted in your home that can be displayed as wall art that will serve as a reminder to everyone in your home. I will be creating examples of these wall arts in the myproverbs31family shop. If you will like notification for once they are ready, be sure to sign up to the bonuses page-myproverbs31family.com/POP31bonuses.

5.   Music and worship

A very important factor that is usually missed is the role music plays in a person's life or home. I know of a young boy who had Christian parents but strayed and ended up always in trouble at school and took part in criminal activities, including drug dealing. On spending time with this family, I found out this young boy was addicted to Tupac and other rap music and listened to it all hours of the day. It was hardly surprising the path he took, even though his parents were devout Christians.

In 2018, London's police commissioner cited drill rap as a factor behind a rapid rise in knife crime in the capital.[20]

Ladies, you must be aware of the type of music that is being played in your home. Music is a source of entertainment but is also a spiritual tool used to invoke both good and bad spirits, ambience, or energy into homes. It is therefore important to be mindful of the type of music being played in your home. Personally, I mostly only play gospel and worship music in my home. I will say, as a rule of thumb, one can generally know what type of energy a

---

[20] The Sciences: The Curious Case of Drill Rap and its Link to Violent Crime, 17 April 2020 [Link]

particular music brings by the words of the songs and the artists' values or lifestyle.

6.   Wisdom

I like Cambridge Dictionary's definition of wisdom which is the ability to use your knowledge and experience to make good decisions and judgements. I like even better this Bible's definition, "the wisdom of God is first pure, then peaceable, gentle, willing to yield, full of mercy and good fruits, without partiality and without hypocrisy."[21]

Scriptures tell us that there is godly wisdom, and devilish wisdom. Evil wisdom propagates chaos and confusion in the home, while godly wisdom enables us to display characters that help build a home, character that is peaceful and drama-free, gentle, yielding, submissive, merciful, and gracious.

Wisdom is the most important tool a woman needs to turn her house into a haven of peace, harmony and tranquility.

It takes godly wisdom to know when to be quiet on a matter for the sake of peace, and when and how to speak so that our words will yield peace and solution. It takes wisdom to put out fires and resolve disputes that will inevitably happen in our homes rather than escalate matters. It takes wisdom to support your spouse and children when they face challenges and to influence them to be better and not bitter. It takes wisdom to know how to be influential by being kind, gentle and sometimes quiet, rather than nagging and insisting on having things your way. Wisdom is required to manage all the demands on your time and to know what to prioritise, delay, delegate or ignore. It takes wisdom to keep a beautiful home and keep it clean. It takes wisdom to stay happily married.

The good news is that while we are not all born with the wisdom for homemaking, we are promised that if we lack wisdom and ask God, the author of all good wisdom, He will give us generously. Let me repeat that. Ask God for wisdom and he promises to give it generously.

Let us pray:

---

[21] Bible, James 3:17

Scripture Recitation

If any of you lack wisdom, you should ask God, who gives generously to all without finding fault, and it will be given to you.

-JAMES 1:5

Then my people will live in a peaceful habitation, And in secure dwellings and in undisturbed resting places.

ISAIAH 32:18

This is what the LORD says: "'I will restore the fortunes of Jacob's tents and have compassion on his dwellings...; Out of them shall come songs of thanksgiving, and the voices of those who celebrate. I will multiply them, and they shall not be few; I will make them honored, and they shall not be small.

JEREMIAH 30:18-19

Peace be within your walls and security within your towers!

PSALMS 122:7

By wisdom a house is built, and by understanding it is established; by knowledge the rooms are filled with all precious and pleasant riches.

PROVERBS 24:3-4

For jealousy and selfishness are not God's kind of wisdom. Such things are earthly, unspiritual, and demonic. But the wisdom from above is first of all pure. It is also peace-loving, gentle at all times, and willing to yield to others. It is full of mercy and the fruit of good deeds. It shows no favouritism and is always sincere.

JAMES 3:15,17

Prayers

1. Lord, I thank You that with Your help, my home is a haven of peace, love, joy, and laughter.

2. I welcome Your presence and spirit, Your kingdom, righteousness, joy, peace, fun, laughter, and celebration into my home.

3. Be the head and builder of my home, Lord.

4. Lord, I ask, please give me the wisdom of God, that is peaceful, submissive, understanding, gentle, merciful, and forgiving.

5. Take away from me or any member of my household the behaviour and characters that are contentious, quarrelsome, nagging, controlling, and full of drama.

6. I welcome into my home the spirit and characters of love, unity, joy, peace, patience, kindness, goodness, gentleness, understanding, honour, and respect.

7. Drive away from my home, in Jesus' mighty name and by the blood of Jesus, the spirit of division, gossiping, confusion, quarrelling spirits, and selfishness.

8. Fill every member of my home with love, understanding, and honour for one another.

9. May every member and visitor of this household experience sound sleep, rest, peace, and comfort in my home.

10. May there be the sound of laughter, merriness, and fun within my borders.

11. I receive grace, discipline, wisdom and help to keep my home tidy, clean, and beautiful always.

12. I have easy access to items that will make my home look and smell beautiful.

13. My home is filled with quiet, serenity, treasures, creativity, intelligence, healing, and God's presence, in Jesus' name.

14. My home is a haven of peace, rest, kindness, joy, laughter, healing and anointing that is tangibly felt by every resident and visitor.

Day 12

SUPERNATURAL CHILDBIRTH

Your children rise and call you blessed; your husband also, and he praises you.

- Proverbs 31:28

When man and woman were created, they were blessed to multiply, expand, rule, and have dominion over the earth through childbearing. While both men and women are needed for procreation, women, however, are the life-givers in that they carry the womb—the environment through which seed (sperm and egg) is planted, nurtured, grows and is born. A man's legacy and inheritance are not fully realised or passed on through his bloodline without a woman.

The womb, being an environment of life and growth, was never originally designed to be a place of death through miscarriage or abortion; neither was it originally designed to be unproductive. If a womb does not produce children, or continually miscarries the zygote or embryo that is growing during childbearing age, then there is a defect. It is, therefore, important that as women we don't take a healthy womb for granted and thank God regularly for the miracle of our womb and pray that any defects in the womb will be healed so that our wombs will be a wholesome environment through which children are conceived, nurtured, and born, if children are what we desire.

I take this moment to send love, empathy, and good thoughts to you if you are going through a hard time with childbirth or have experienced barrenness, miscarriage, or any other issues with your womb. I pray that our God of healing and comfort will touch you as you read through this chapter and hold you in His loving embrace. May He give you strength and restore hope and joy where hope was lost.

At this point, I think it is important to discuss spiritual wombs and spiritual or non-biological children. I believe all women are mothers, either biologically or spiritually, through the lives you impact. Your spiritual womb is the place where non-biological children, businesses, inventions, and ideas are conceived, protected, and grown, before being born into reality. Your clients, mentees, disciples, and people whose lives you impact and transform, also make up your spiritual children. This fact gave me hope and purpose when I had no biological children. I want every woman, irrespective of whether you have biological children or not, to derive a sense of pride and appreciation for your spiritual children. After all, scripture says, "many are the children of the barren."[22]

Supernatural childbirth

The supernatural childbirth experience was made popular by Jackie Mize and her husband who gave birth to five children miraculously pain and sickness free, after being told that they would never have children. Many women have since shared testimonials about their supernatural childbirth experiences after applying the principles Jackie shared in her book, "Supernatural Childbirth." Some of these stories include painless pregnancies and birth experiences, tear-free pregnancies, home births, and giving birth after serious medical issues, and negative doctors' reports. All forms of childbearing is feminine, miraculous and worth celebrating. However, I usually refer to the supernatural method of giving birth as feminine childbirth because this method of childbearing is a lot easier, effortless, pain and labour free compared to normal childbirth experiences most women have.

Irrespective of your experiences in relation to childbirth and having children, may you experience restored hope and miraculous childbirths.

Warning, some of the Prayers below may sound ridiculous, unrealistic, and maybe triggering, but for those who desire and believe in supernatural childbirth experiences, it is very possible as attested by many stories from

---

[22] Bible, Isaiah 54:1

around the world. Pray the Prayers below repeatedly as an act of faith. It's also worth reiterating that any form of childbirth (painful or pain-free) is miraculous and worthy of gratitude. Please do write to me and share your testimonials. Let us pray:

Scripture Recitation

He settles the barren woman in a home, making her the joyous mother of children. Praise the Lord!

PSALMS 113:9

Behold, children are a heritage from the Lord, the fruit of the womb a reward.

PSALMS 127:3

No woman in your land will miscarry or be barren; I will fulfil the number of her days.

EXODUS 23:26

Yes, You have been with me from birth; from my mother's womb, You have cared for me. No wonder I am always praising You!

PSALM 71:6

I will say to the north, 'Give them up!' and to the south, 'Do not hold them back!' Bring My sons from afar, and My daughters from the ends of the earth

ISAIAH 43:6

Prayers

1. Thank you, God, that my womb is blessed and whole.

2. Thank you, Lord, for the gift of a womb and for the blessing and miracle of childbearing and procreation.

3. Thank you that all good and perfect gifts come from. You and Your blessings make rich without adding sorrows. May I experience the joy of childbirth.

4. I cover my womb, ovaries, and fallopian tubes in the blood of Jesus.

5. My womb will function as it was originally designed to, an environment for fruitfulness, safety, and growth for my baby during the pregnancy season.

6. My womb will bear fruit and give birth to healthy, happy, and wholesome children.

7. My womb will not reject or kill my children.

8. I receive wisdom and grace to take the right diet and actions to keep a healthy womb.

9. I am healed and free from fibroids, polyps, endometriosis, fibroids, cancer, or any defects causing barrenness, miscarriages, stillborn babies, or unhealthy babies.

10. I pray for a healthy and beautiful baby who will grow healthily.

11. I will be one of those who glow, thrive, and become more beautiful and attractive inside and out during and post pregnancy with ease.

12. I plead the blood of Jesus and cry out for mercy about any actions of mine or my partner, our parents, and forefathers, that may have led to barrenness or complications.

13. Thank you, that we are already forgiven, and free us from all iniquities that are having a negative effect on me or my family by the blood of Jesus [mention any that come to mind as you pray; examples could include abortion, child sacrifice, child abuse or murder, idol worship etc]

14. I am free from any guilt, shame, or self-blame that I experience in Jesus name.

15. I pray and I thank you for supernatural pregnancy and childbirth where my pregnancy and childbirth process will be pain and sickness free for me and my baby.

16. There will be no complications throughout my pregnancy process. There will be no pain, sickness, excess, or unhealthy weight-gain.

17. I will not experience any negative, or ugly face changes or bloating.

18. I pray against unhealthy cravings and undesirable weight gain during pregnancy.

19. During my pregnancy, I will detest unhealthy foods, refined, sugary or weight-gaining foods, and everything bad for me and my baby during and after pregnancy. Rather, I will begin to crave healthy vegetables, water, ginger, greens, lemon, and healthy food during and after pregnancy.

20. My diet, exercise, sleep, and lifestyle habits will change for the better during and after pregnancy (this is not to say I won't start making healthy changes from now, but things will significantly get even better and easier during pregnancy).

21. I will glow and become more beautiful, attractive and at a healthier, more desirable weight during and after pregnancy.

Prayer for spiritual wombs, and non-biological children such as adopted, foster, or other types of children

22. I pray also for my spiritual womb that it is blessed and will be productive.

23. I give birth to healthy and wholesome spiritual children, disciples, mentees, clients, dreams, visions, and ideas.

24. I grow in impact and influence

25. Connect me with my tribe, disciples, clients, followers non-biological children from near and far, those who I will impact their lives.

26. Connect me Lord with my God-ordained children and families, in Jesus' name. We will be a match made in heaven and settle well into each other's lives.

27. May I be filled with God's love, care, and protection for my child, and may my husband and I be the perfect parents for our child/children.

Day 13

YOUR JOURNAL AND PERSONAL NOTES

Which of the themes discussed from the last 12 days resonates most with you, and which aspects will you intentionally work on?

What is the Lord telling you to do and what actions will you take to meet your goals and desires for yourself? [list actions and put realistic dates by which you will do them]

SECTION 2

PRAYERS FOR YOUR HUSBAND, HIS MANHOOD AND MASCULINITY

Day 14

A MAN'S CAPACITY

Be strong and become a man!

- 1 Kings 2:2-4

Capacity refers to the maximum amount an object can hold. In human terms capacity is a good measure of how much of a good thing a person can handle given their character, knowledge, skills, experience, and track record. Capacity is what employers or certifiers consider before offering employment, promotion, or qualifications to ensure that a person is not given responsibilities, opportunities or gifts that may end up being detrimental to the person and others due to limited capacity. It's the same for men. A man needs to expand his capacity to become a good husband and be given the gift of a good wife and family without the risk of destroying himself, his wife, his family, or society at large.

So, what does the capacity of a man have to do with women? Firstly, as a wise woman, you need to vet and verify a man's capacity for you, your purpose and legacy before you commit to him. Secondly, you, as a wise woman, have a role to influence the men in your life through Prayers and feminine influence.

The instruction to pray for men came at a time I felt I was too wounded to be married. As I began to negotiate with God to allow me to enjoy companionship through dating multiple men who were at least decent enough to date, the Lord showed me another perspective as to why I, and many other good women were not married, through the story of King Caleb in the Bible.

When Othniel approached king Caleb to marry his daughter, he requested that Othniel could have his daughter after he fought and won a battle against a very strong national enemy.[23] As I was meditating on Othniel and the calibre of man he had to be, mentally, physically, emotionally, relationally, and even materially, to firstly, accept the challenge to risk his life, and then fight and win a war with a whole nation, for a wife, I was blown away.

Aside from Othniel, there are many men in the Bible who had to pay a very high bride price that could cost them their lives and some cases did. Best of all, Jesus' high price for his bride was a very painful and torturous death on the cross for our sins.

God spoke to me very clearly as I read Othniel's story and I was negotiating with God about dating. He said to me, "if an earthly king required such a high price before he gave his daughter away in marriage, what makes you think I will give my daughter, in whom I have invested so much, away so cheaply?"

There is a tribe of women who are of very high value reading this. You are a dream wife and have all it takes to make a man happy. God has invested heavily in you. You have taken time to heal, grow, and elevate your character, health, body, and spirituality. Rather than giving yourself to men and temporary relationships, you separated and consecrated yourself for purity and holiness.

You, like I did, have begun to feel that all this work and purity may be in vain as you see others 'less worthy' than you in happy marriages. You, dear daughter, are worthy of nothing less than a fitting king. Like King Caleb, there is, however, a very high price for your hand in marriage. God showed me that there is a capacity men must reach, battles they must win, in order to be worthy of God's high-value daughters as He will not be selling His daughters for less, to men who don't have the capacity to love, cherish, and

---

[23] Bible, Judges 1:12-13

protect them. The same is true if you are a good woman in an unhappy marriage. This means your husband's capacity is limited.

A clarion call has gone out for a generation of men who will grow up, man up, level up, and build their capacity as men worthy of God's high-priced jewels. These men need to increase their capacity—grow in their relationship with God, their manhood, and character, so that they can be strong enough to overcome battles, to pursue, protect, provide, and pay the price required for God's gift of a good wife.

The good news is that with prayer, ordinary men can be activated to become kings and champions worthy of God's high-priced jewels. Precious one, your Prayers for your present or future husband, and men at large, can cause a generation of men to be activated to be kings worthy of you and your sisters. The Lord told me that Prayers and activation of men is needed to ensure that many of His daughters get married and remain happily married.

In this section, we will be praying for men to build capacity in the areas of leadership, spirituality, love, finance, mental and emotional intelligence. A loving father will only give away his most prized jewels to men with the capacity to love and lead them.

Let us pray:

Scripture Recitation

Now Jabez called on the God of Israel, saying, "Oh that You would bless me indeed and enlarge my capacity, and that Your hand might be with me, ..." And God granted him what he requested.

1 CHRONICLES 4:10

A wise man is full of strength, and a man of knowledge enhances his might, for by wise guidance you can wage your war, and in abundance of counsellors there is victory.

PROVERBS 24:5-6

Prayers

1. Lord, deal with my husband and the men in my life. Enlarge his capacity in every area of life—manhood, masculinity, leadership, and in character.

2. Help his mindset and help him to know that he is a champion, and I am the prize he must pursue, woo and love.

3. Help him to win the battle and warfare required for him to attain his purpose, promise, and purpose mate.

4. Enlarge his capacity to be ready to receive, afford, protect, and love Your high-priced investment and gift to him—his wife, family, purpose, and empire.

5. Help him to be battle-ready always and to overcome every test life throws at him.

6. Enlarge his leadership capacity. May he lead in love, serve, and be a great example for his family, children, and the people God has called him to.

7. Strengthen his relationship, love for, union with, submission, and obedience to the Lord and may he submit to correct and godly leadership.

8. Remove every wrong relationship and negative influence in his life.

9. Give him direction, clarity, and vision in line with Your purpose and destiny for his life. Remove all confusion and indecision from him.

10. Enlarge his love capacity and his ability to speak his wife's and family's love language without fatigue.

11. May he find joy, ease, and purpose in loving his wife (me) in these areas [emphasise areas that are important to you]:

- Pursuit
- Quality time
- Meaningful conversations and encouragement
- Thoughtful, meaningful, creative and luxurious gifts
- Acts of service
- Affection
- Touch
- Provision
- Protection
- Presence
- Intellect

12. Lord, deliver him from laziness and weariness in love.

13. Strengthen him in his inner self. He is strong in mind, spirit, and body.

14. He is equipped and grow in the following areas necessary to win spiritual, mental, and physical battles:

- Salvation, winning beliefs and mindset
- Righteousness and holiness
- Truth, integrity, transparency, and honesty
- Faith and confidence
- God word and truthful ideologies

15. Thank you, Lord, that You are enlarging the capacity of his mind and You help him to overcome the battles against his mind and mindset.

16. Lord, heal and deliver him from:

- Pride and excessive ego
- Destructive competition
- Low self-esteem
- Disappointment and despair
- Hopelessness
- Hard and cold-heartedness
- Stubbornness
- Anger

- o   Unforgiveness
- o   Misunderstanding
- o   Malice or silent treatment
- o   Laziness
- o   Addictions
- o   Narcissism and personality disorders

17. He is a champion and wins every battle for his mind with the help of God.

18. He is healed from all mental health issues such as:

- o   Anger
- o   Offense
- o   Bitterness
- o   Depression
- o   Unforgiveness
- o   Anxiety
- o   Workaholism
- o   Schizophrenia
- o   Psychosis
- o   Psycho Affective Disorder

19. Give him the desire, drive, and direction to proactively work on healing his issues and growing his capacity.

20. Fill him, oh Lord, with a heart of:

- o   Love
- o   Light
- o   Understanding
- o   Forgiveness
- o   Generosity
- o   Humility
- o   Kindness
- o   Wisdom

21. Help him overcome the battle of temptation and sins, including:

- o   Alcoholism

- o Workaholism
- o Pornography
- o Sexual immorality
- o Prideful ego
- o Addictions

22. Thank you, Lord, for answering my Prayers. Before I call, You answer me, while I am still speaking, You hear me. (Isaiah 65:24)

Day 15

BOYS TO MEN—AWAKEN THE

SLEEPING MAN

How long will you lie down, O sluggard? When will you arise from your sleep?

- Proverbs 6:9

This section is about awakening men's manhood so that they elevate in spirit, soul, and body, from boys to men, kids to kings, single to husbands, players to pilots. We use sleep as a metaphor to describe men who are not awake, aware, or conscious in the following areas of manhood:

1.   **His purpose in life**

A man sleeping in his purpose is someone who is unfulfilled in his job or life. He lacks passion and is unaware of what his contribution to this world is, and the purpose for which he was created. He usually lacks direction and focus and ends up working for another man's purpose, for money and to survive, while extremely unfulfilled in the process.

2.   **The need for a wife and committed relationship**

A man who is asleep to his need for a wife is the type of man who is very content sleeping around, juggling different women without settling with one, or perhaps he is even content to remain single after his thirties or even forties or the rest of his life. He may even commit or cohabit with one woman but not see the need for marriage. If, after reading this, you are saying to yourself, "what is wrong with cohabiting?" then you too are sleeping.

I am very shocked at the growing Red Pill movement that views marriage and commitment as a disadvantage to men. Men who are committed to love one wife are often ridiculed as "simps" or "beta males." It is sad to witness Christian men adopting these views, many of whom are divorced or wounded from past relationships. While it is true that there are people called to live a single and fulfilled life, and there is a very beneficial season of singleness in every person's life, most people are not called to be single after a period of time. For people who are not called to be single forever, or people who desire a spouse sexually or emotionally, there comes a time when it's no longer good to be alone, especially if being single too long goes on to affect whether you can have a child. This is the time when "two is better than one."[24]

3.   The identity and character of his wife

A man asleep completely overlooks a woman who is wife material. He is more mesmerised by looks and skin colour over character. Many of you are good women reading this and have been in situations where a man was completely oblivious to your worth and ignored or even mistreated you. We have all heard of or experienced situations where a man later becomes attracted to a lady after he has overlooked her for years. In this scenario, the man is said to have woken up from his sleep. I watched a story of a couple who were friends and had a strong attraction for one another. They did not act on it and went their separate ways and eventually married different people. Many years later, they had both divorced from their spouses when they randomly crossed each other's path. They are now married! I wonder how much time and heartache they would have saved if the man made a move the first time.

For some of these sleeping men, they wake up when it is too late. The woman is taken by the time he wakes up and, in some cases, he is not able to find a woman as good as the one he let go of. He is now forced to settle for less.

4.   His responsibilities and masculinity

---

[24] Bible, Ecclesiastes 4:9

A man is sleeping when he is oblivious to what it means to be a man, or to his responsibilities as a man and husband, to God, family, and society. These are the type of men who neglect their family, and when they are present, they are almost good for nothing. These men adopt the feminine or "receiver" position in their relationships while their women are the providers, hustlers, leaders, and spiritual covering of the home.

I know a man who wasted his youth. He dropped out of school, with no education or work, he stayed at home taking money from his father for basics such as transport, and wondered why he couldn't find a woman. He was fast asleep!

5. Spiritual connection with God

A man's biggest and most common downfall is pride. Pride is when a man believes he knows it all and is accountable to only himself. He tells God who God is, and that is "self,". He worships himself. It takes humility and strength to acknowledge and submit to God.

Furthermore, a masculine man, as the leader of the home, should be the spiritual covering of his home. This means he is connected to God, prays regularly for his family, leads, and teaches them spiritual and practical life principles. If you are reading this thinking your spirituality or connection to the true God isn't necessary and the divine is all about self, then it means you need to wake up from your slumber before it is too late. A man who isn't aware of his need for God is not only sleeping but the scripture describes him as dead. We are ultimately spirit beings with a soul and a body. Our spirits were originally designed to connect with God, our Creator. While it's important to take care of your health, financial and emotional needs, it is most important to meet your spiritual needs as this is the only part of you that lives on and determines where you will be for eternity.

There are three types of awakenings that need to happen to a man who is sleeping:

Spiritual awakening

Spiritual awakening, also known as revival, is when a person's spirit comes alive through God's spirit, just like when you jumpstart a dead car battery by connecting it with another car that is fully charged. Similarly, awakening results in change in the recipient, both personally and in a nation. During the 1904 Welsh Revival, there were several reports of many positive societal changes such as stark reductions in alcoholism rates, closures of sex saloons, lower crime rates, and other positive changes.[25] More recently, and closer to home, in 2020 Vivian Rose started a prayer event for men, the same time I felt a nudge from the Lord to call a prayer for husbands again in 2020. In Vivien's prayer group, she released a prophetic word about revival for men. She said that an avalanche of men would be released from prison. Amazingly, months later, that same year all around the world, the news broadcasted mass releases of men from prisons in Massachusetts. That same year, there were also prison breaks in Nigeria and mass releases from prisons in other parts of the world. These are the sort of events that happen for individuals and the masses when there is spiritual awakening.

Enlightenment

Enlightenment happens to our soul or mind when a person becomes aware or gains understanding and clarity. A man is enlightened when he gains clarity around his purpose, responsibilities, and his and his family's spiritual, mental, and physical needs as a man.

Another important level of enlightenment is wisdom. Wisdom is gaining and applying knowledge, truths, or information correctly. It is great to be enlightened or gain knowledge about something. However, this is only helpful when applied in the right context and at the right time. Wisdom helps us know how, when, and where to apply a given piece of information or not.

Let us pray:

---

[25] The Legacy of The Welsh Revival 1904-1905, Patrick Slater https://www.methodistevangelicals.org.uk/Articles/523541/The_Legacy_of.as px

Scripture Recitation

Awake, O sleeper, rise up from the dead and Christ will give you light. So be careful how you live. Don't live like fools, but like those who are wise.

EPHESIANS 5:14

Then the angel who was speaking with me returned and roused me, as a man who is awakened from his sleep.

ZECHARIAH 4:1

My prayer is that light will flood your hearts and you will understand the hope given to you when God chose you. Then you will discover the glorious blessings that will be yours together with all God's people.

EPHESIANS 1:17-18

Your dead will live; Their corpses will rise. You who lie in the dust, awake and shout for joy, For your dew is as the dew of the dawn, And the earth will give birth to the departed spirits.

ISAIAH 26:19

According to the riches of His glory, you will be strengthened by His spirit in your inner being.

EPHESIANS 3:16

Prophesy to the dry bones and say, "oh, dry bones hear the word of the Lord."

EZEKIAL 37:4

Prayers

1. Lord, I submit to Your spirit [mention his name], wake him up and grow him in every area that he is asleep.

2. Humble him, Lord, and lead him to the realisation of his need for God and to submission to the rock that is higher than he, the rock of ages, the rock of pure, living water, the rock of wisdom and knowledge, the rock that quenches his thirsty soul.

3. Breathe in him the breath of life and send Your words of truth to his spirit, his soul, his mind, and his ear.

4. The power of life and death is in my words, so I prophesy and speak life to all of him, his soul, body, mind, brain cells, awake! Wake up, rise and shine!

5. Husband awake and grow in your spiritual connection to God. Come to the realisation of your purpose, responsibilities, needs, and purpose relationships.

6. Let every dead part of you—spirit, soul, body, brain, mind, and cells, wake up, rise up and shine.

7. Let your ears hear fully and your spiritual eyes see fully truth in all areas of life.

8. Be strengthened and quickened with God's power, and Holy spirit in your innermost being—your spirit, soul, mind, heart, and brain.

9. I speak death to every part of you or your character that is negative.

10. Lord take away from him every negative thought pattern, belief system, culture, upbringing and way of thinking that is not in line with his best self.

11. He is the best leader, the best man, the best father, the best friend, confidant, servant, businessman, colleague, and mentor I know.

12. He is an example to the world around him and he leaves a great legacy for the current generation and generations unborn.

13. Give him the will and desire to do the right thing at the right times in every area of his life—at home, work, business, and in his relationships.

14. Let the light of Your truth, knowledge, understanding, insight, and wisdom shine on every area of his life, including his:

   - Spirituality
   - Finance
   - Love
   - Marriage
   - Fatherhood
   - Relationships
   - Friendships
   - Responsibilities
   - Business
   - Career
   - Purpose

Day 16

A MAN OF PURPOSE

And we know that God causes everything to work together for the good of those who love God and are called according to His purpose for them.

- Romans 8:28

Purpose is defined as the reason why something exists. Purpose is especially important for men because a man needs to know where he is going in life to be a competent husband and leader. A man with a clear purpose is driven and shows up differently in the world and in a relationship. He is not only able to effectively choose a spouse and make relationship decisions aligned with purpose, but he is also better able to provide leadership and direction to his family if he has clear goals he is working towards. Men without drive or purpose are a nightmare for purposeful feminine women.

The story of Joseph in the Bible details his journey to purpose. Many lessons can be gleaned from his story about purpose.

Joseph came from a decent home where he was loved by his father but through sibling rivalry and the jealousy of his brothers, he was sold into slavery and went through a life of ups and very low downs. He ended up in prison for many years but eventually made it to his purpose, where he became the most respected and highest- ranking person of his day—the second-in-command to the King. The president, his countrymen, and people from around the world, came to Joseph for solutions to problems and crises facing the whole world at the time. It was after reaching purpose that Joseph connected with his wife.

The fight for his dream

At the beginning of Joseph's story we are told that Joseph had a dream, and, "when he told it to his brothers, they hated him even more"[26]

Joseph attracted the hatred of his brothers because of his dreams. The plot for his murder and rejection from his family began at the point where he had a dream and spoke about it. He was then sold into slavery and went on to face much opposition, hatred, false accusations, and temptations and eventually he was imprisoned for a crime he didn't commit.

Many men destined for greatness start where Joseph started, with a dream, a vision, good academic and career prospects. However, they attract a lot of opposition, jealousy, hatred, and rejection through life because of their purpose. These men start off with very good prospects, which are short-lived due to so many challenges— from drug and alcohol issues, to suicides, mental health problems, crime, gang memberships, pornography, sex addiction, stabbing, bullying, discrimination, illness, and the list goes on and on. All these problems many men face are assassination attempts on their lives and purpose. Sadly, most men don't win the fight and either die before their time or their dreams, manhood, and purpose die.

'Strike the shepherd and the sheep scatter'. If men fulfilled their purpose and took their position in the family as the heads, shepherds, providers and protectors of their homes, a lot of ailments society faces wouldn't be.

Joseph's success formula for purpose

Despite Joseph's oppositions and suffering through life, he made it to purpose where he was successful, recognised, productive, and married. Unknown to him, his downfalls, disappointment, and suffering all worked out to position him for purpose. All things really do work out for the good of those who are on their purpose path.[27]

---

[26] 28 Bible, Genesis 37:5,8
[27] Bible, Romans 8:28 [Paraphrased]

The secret of his successes can be found in Genesis,[28] where we are told when he was in the house of one of his slave masters: "**The Lord was with Joseph**, and he became a successful man … His master saw that the Lord was with him and that **the Lord caused all that he did to succeed in his hands**. So, Joseph found favour in his sight, and he made him overseer and put him in charge of all…" This was repeated when he went to the prison where he was recognised, put in charge, and eventually invited to work at the palace.

"Joseph's Success Formula" was the God factor—God was with him, and he had a close friendship with God, and walked in righteousness. This friendship with God resulted in him having favour with people and being successful in all his projects, providing solutions and innovations for major problems and challenges of his day.

Connection with God is like a phone connected to a charger or power source. It needs to regularly connect to stay alive and get recharged for performance. Similarly, our men need to be connected to God to gain the strength to overcome adversity. Praying for our men's relationship with God is so vital for their manhood and purpose. Many men would have died but for the fact that God is with them. Many of them make it to greatness despite so many challenges, because of God's favour over them.

Promotion for purpose

Joseph's journey to purpose can be summarised in this one scripture. "The stone that the builders rejected has become the chief cornerstone."

Many great men of purpose, especially those aligned with God, will always face extreme rejection in their lives. Joseph was rejected by his brothers. David was rejected by his family and wasn't even mentioned when his father was asked to present his children. Jesus faced immense rejection and persecution by the very people He created, healed, and helped. These great men, however, did not allow rejection to disqualify them from purpose, but used it as a stepping stone and drive to reach greatness.

---

[28] Bible, Genesis 39:2-4,21-23

Recognition and reward

It's worth noting that despite Joseph's standout success, his trailblazing ideas and solutions, he needed to be recognised, remembered, recommended, and rewarded for his good work to break out from the prison to the palace. Like Joseph, our men can overcome rejection and reach the palace, the place of prominence, power, and purpose through God's help and favour from people who will not reject them but remember their good works, recommend them and reward them. May God repackage and reintroduce our men to those who wrote them off. May God heal them in areas of their rejection and cause them to be remembered and rewarded for their good work.

Let us pray:

Scripture Recitation

Joseph is a fruitful bough, a fruitful bough by a spring; his branches run over the wall. The archers bitterly attacked him, shot at him, and harassed him severely, yet his bow remained unmoved; his arms were made agile by the hands of the Mighty One of Jacob, by the God of your Father who will help you, by the one who will bless you with blessings of heaven above.

GENESIS 49:22-25

The LORD will fulfil his purpose for me; Your steadfast love, O LORD, endures forever. Do not forsake the work of Your hands.

PSALM 138:8

For it is God who works in you to will and to act in order to fulfill his good purpose

PHILLIPIANS 2:13

And we know that in all things God works for the good of those who love him, who have been called according to his purpose

ROMANS 8:28

Many are the plans in the mind of a man, but it is the purpose of the LORD that will stand

PROVERBS 19:21

Prayers

1. Thank you that as we commit our ways to You, You direct our paths.

2. I commit [mention specific names of men you are praying for]. Give him dreams and vision that are in line with Your purpose for his life.

3. Guide him along his purpose path that in his business, work, ministry friendships, relationships, and all areas of life, he will be in God's perfect will and purpose for his life.

4. Like Paul was redirected to make a U-turn for purpose through a special encounter with God, may my husband have a special encounter that will open his eyes, heart, and align his feet for God's purpose for his life.

5. Let his ears hear, and his eyes see Your direction clearly in every junction of his life, and deliver him from deceit and temptation.

6. Help him obey and act on Your directions and instructions.

7. Let every dream killer that attempts to take my husband's life or make it miserable because of God's purpose for his life fail, in Jesus' name.

8. Like Joseph, may everything work out for his good and for God's purpose for his life, in Jesus' name.

9. I pray against the following dream killers which have robbed many men of their destinies:

   o Rejection and hatred from parents
   o Rejection, envy, betrayal, and hatred from family and friends
   o Suicide
   o Gang and knife crime
   o Untimely death
   o Wrong associations and friendships

- Slavery, restrictions, and post-slavery syndrome
- False accusation, lies, gossip, and negative whispers
- Spiritual abuse
- Physical abuse and imprisonment
- Narcissism
- Pride, ego, and stubbornness
- Sexual abuse, including adultery, fornication, promiscuity, and rape
- Rebellion and disobedience
- Sin and temptations, including sexual sin, addiction, abuse, anger, and others

10. Lord, give him the desire to acknowledge Your presence with him, honour You and draw near to You as his Maker, Father, and close Friend.

11. Let Your tangible presence be with him, and may he recognise, honour, and engage with Your presence to the extent that people will recognise that God is with him.

12. May he hear the voice of God clearly.

13. May Your favour be with him and make all his efforts very successful.

14. May he grow in favour with God and men.

15. Help him to be successful to the extent that he can't be ignored but is recognised, promoted, and put in charge of prominent projects and programmes in line with purpose.

16. The prison gates are open, and he is free from every spiritual, mental, or physical imprisonment.

17. He shatters, smashes, and breaks free from all imprisonments, glass ceilings, spiritual bars, iron membranes, limitations, handicaps, impediments, and discriminations.

18. He will no longer be stereotyped, marginalised, stigmatised, immobilised, terrorised, characterised, criticised, censored, misjudged, mishandled, or mismanaged[29].

19. He is impactful. Enlarge his territory and increase his influence and impact

20. He is the head and not the tail, at the fore and not behind, excellent, and not mediocre, a leader, shepherd, provider, and protector of his home.

21. Lord, have mercy on him and reimburse him of all that he has lost through false accusation, imprisonments, delays, and denials.

22. May he experience double rewards for his troubles and expose his accusers.

23. Repackage him and reintroduce him to those who wrote him off, for Your glory.

24. May he be remembered, recommended, and rewarded. His good works, ideas, innovations, and kindnesses not be forgotten but instead be rehearsed to the people who will facilitate his purpose and prosperity.

25. Activate his God-given gifts and talents and let them bring him before kings.

26. Lord, help our men experience divine promotion, like Joseph, from rejected to relevant, from neglected to needed, imprisonment to purpose, from prison to the palace.

27. Let it be said of him, like Jesus, that the stone the builders rejected has become the chief cornerstone.

28. Like Joseph, give him wisdom to solve the problems of his world. Power, authority, success, creativity, innovative ideas, ingenuity, inventions, and connections overflow from him.

---

[29] Adapted from Cindy Trimm's Atomic Prayers

Day 17

HIS MENTAL HEALTH

This is what the Lord, the God of your father David, says: "I have heard your prayer and seen your tears; I will heal you."

- 2 Kings 20:5

Many men jump from one relationship to the next, one traumatic event to the next, in and out of marriages and relationships, completely broken-hearted and hardened. This man whose heart has been broken repeatedly without taking time out to heal loses his ability to bond, love, and connect with his wife. He sabotages good relationships while damaging himself, his spouse, children, and generations unborn.

Ultimately, some of these wounded men end up on the "Men Going Their Own Way" (MGTOW) train. You will find these men on YouTube making a living from tearing women down and discouraging men from getting married. Unfortunately, these misogynists attract many other men who have been equally wounded, and then indoctrinate them with very relationship-damaging ideologies.

Love heals

Healing is needed for our men. The process of healing is extensive and can take time.

Love is the most effective medicine for men's wounded souls. Love is kind, patient, gentle and a lot of nice things, but for the purpose of praying effectively for the men and husbands in your lives, I feel led to focus on a particular type of love that will work on men. This type of love is seldom spoken about in today's world filled with emasculated, feminine men. This type of love hurts at first and feels like hate, but actually results in healing and growth in the long term. I am referring to loving discipline.

I believe today's modern men need to be disciplined out of their extreme femininity and wounds. The Bible says that the hearts of men are desperately wicked[30] which means that by virtue of our humanity, men's hearts are naturally wicked. Furthermore, God's people were repeatedly told throughout scripture to circumcise their hearts to be able to love.[31] It is interesting that the word circumcise was used for men. Circumcision is a very painful process of removing skin from a man's genitals. Circumcision of the heart, I believe, refers to the pain of discipline that leads to a changed heart.

I know a very hardened man who was very wounded and betrayed by his family. As a result, he wronged his beautiful wife and family through cheating, abandonment, and abuse. He had zero remorse and justified his wrongs. After many years, after this man hit rock bottom in life, he turned to God, through intense consecration, prayer and repentance to get him out of a "dead end" situation in his life. To my surprise, this man changed while in his fifties, and asked many people he had offended for forgiveness. He got to the point of zero where he had no choice but to repent. Many were surprised, as he was known as the most stubborn and hot-headed person in the family. Life taught him a lesson and I believe if he hadn't hit rock bottom, he would have got worse. Through that experience I realised that for some people, especially men who are stubborn, maybe for all of us, life has to teach us lessons before we experience a change of heart. For men who are stubborn, oblivious, and unremorseful, they especially will need to hit the wall, encounter an experience that will force them to begin to consider their ways, heal and change. Many single people, for example, who desire a godly spouse, as they get older, are forced to address themselves and make changes necessary to get married. This type of suffering that works for our improvement is described in scripture as the "discipline of the Lord." I

---

[30] Bible, Jeremiah 17:9
[31] Bible, Deuteronomy 30:6

strongly believe many men have been mollycoddled and need to have an encounter with the discipline of the Lord to heal and change their ways.

Let us pray:

Scripture Recitation

Moreover, the Lord your God will circumcise your heart and the heart of your descendants, to love the Lord your God with all your heart and with all your soul, so that you may live.

DEUTERONOMY 30:6

I live in the high and holy place with those whose spirits are contrite and humble. I restore the crushed spirit of the humble and revive the courage of those with repentant hearts.

ISAIAH 57:15

It is for discipline that you endure; God deals with you as with sons; for what son is there whom his father does not discipline? …

All discipline for the moment seems not to be joyful, but sorrowful; yet to those who have been trained by it, afterwards it yields the peaceful fruit of righteousness.

HEBREWS 12:3–11

My son do not despise the LORD'S discipline. Do not resent His rebuke, because the LORD disciples those he loves, as a father the son he delights in.

PROVERBS 3:11-12

Prayers

1. Lord, heal my husband's heart and lead him to the right experiences, people, healers, and counsellors who will facilitate his healing.

2. Heal him in his heart and mind, and from all subconscious and conscious memories that have a negative impact on his life.

3. Circumcise his heart and heal him from:

   o A broken heart
   o Broken trust
   o Rejection
   o Parental neglect
   o A controlling parent
   o Betrayal
   o Users and abusers
   o Abusive parents
   o Abusive and deceptive spiritual leaders
   o Sexual abuse
   o Physical abuse
   o Verbal abuse
   o Negative words
   o Shaming

4. Heal him from his own sins and negative habits.

5. Remove bitterness, pride, unforgiveness, anger, pain, and shame from him.

6. Bring him to his knees. May he change with the "discipline of the Lord."

7. May he grow in love and wisdom through Your discipline with mercy.

8. Humble his ego, pride, and hardened heart, and bring him to healing, repentance and contrition with Your discipline with mercy.

9. Give him a teachable heart so he sees and applies the lessons from every good or bad experience, and becomes a better person as a result.

Day 18

MONEY MATTERS & GENERATIONAL

WEALTH

… Money is the answer to everything.

- Ecclesiastes 10:19

Money matters in marriage. This is confirmed by several studies that show that financial problems are a leading cause of divorce and marital strife.[32]

God's perfect will for His children is abundance and freedom in all areas of our lives, including finances. This is not to say that people don't go through seasons of poverty, financial droughts, and difficulty, but ultimately the goal of every competent man is to work towards overcoming financial droughts and plan towards financial freedom and wealth in the long term.

Financial freedom and abundance, however, start from an abundance mindset. Any wise woman choosing a man should assess his mindset towards money, generosity, and his role as a provider. I have encountered many women who naïvely enter relationships not making proper assessment of their man's financial ambitions and mindset. She is enthusiastic about fulfilling her childhood dream of getting married and doesn't care about the man's money as long as he is a "good" man. Her love is unconditional, and

---

[32] For Richer, for Poorer: Money as a Topic of Marital Conflict in the Home, Lauren M Papp, et al. https://www.ncbi.nlm.nih.gov/pmc/articles/PMC3230928/

she doesn't mind going 50-50 or being the "provider" in the home. In no time after some years in the marriage, she is frustrated, tired, disrespectful, and a huge strain is put on her marriage because of financial constraints. I personally know several divorce and separation cases where this is exactly the story.

The Bible says a competent man is one who leaves an inheritance (wealthy legacy) for his children's children.[33] Financial competency, wealth, and financial literacy is a common way to leave a legacy that will benefit generations after you. However, this happens to those who desire it and have belief systems that align with wealth. It is sad that the 'poverty gospel' where wealth is frowned upon and limitation, sickness and poverty is associated with godliness, is prevalent in many Christian religious circles. Then we wonder why divorce rates and unhappy marriages are prevalent within religious circles.

In his bestseller "Rich Dad Poor Dad," Robert Kiyosaki confirms that one's mindset determines not only their financial destiny but that of their children, too. He compares the various mindsets he learnt from his best friend's rich dad to his poor dad, which led to different financial outcomes for both dads. In learning from his friend's dad and subsequently changing his way of thinking, he was able to break out of generational poverty.

Scripture is very clear that God has already blessed us with all types of blessings spiritually and physically. However only those who have the right mindset, drive and wisdom to access those blessings will make it a reality in their finances and consequently, attain financial freedom.

So why is it important for men to work towards financial freedom, and upgrade their mindset towards wealth, masculine provision, and generosity? Firstly, financial freedom helps a man fulfil his masculine role as the main provider of his household and leave a positive legacy of abundance for his children. Secondly, a man is more likely to align with his purpose and have free time for important things in his life, including his family, when he is financially competent, and not a slave to a job where he works long hours for peanuts. His ability to be generous and loving to his family and serve the world, arrange meaningful dates with his partner, be a better role model for

---

[33] Bible, Proverbs. 13:22

other men, and a more influential person in society increases when he is financially free.

A major benefit of marrying a man at or proactively working towards financial freedom is that you are free from carrying the financial burden of your home, and thus, can more easily rest into your feminine essence. When much or all the financial burden of the home is taken off, you more easily respect, adore and appreciate your man and have more time and energy to put into your relationships, self-care, home, family, passions and feminine business.

Balance

Having said all of the above, if financial freedom is a goal for you, it is important that there is balance. A man who makes a lot of money but is depressed, doesn't make time for his faith, his family, or his purpose, is not financially free, nor a provider but a slave to money, just as a poor man is. As the Bible says, "what does it profit a man to gain the whole world but lose his soul?"[34]

Wealth does, unfortunately, sometimes push people away from God and their loved ones. So, the challenge is striking a balance between managing one's wealth and using it for the greater good of family and society. Having multiple passive streams of income and achieving financial freedom helps a man to be balanced. With God's help, your man's mindset, and your influence, financial freedom and balance are possible to achieve.

Let us pray:

---

[34] Bible, Mark 8:36

Scripture Recitation

But if any man have not care of his own, and especially of those of his house, he hath denied the faith, and is worse than an infidel.

1 TIMOTHY 5:8

You shall remember the LORD your God, for it is He who gives you power to get wealth.

DEUTERONOMY 8:18

Let them shout for joy and be glad, who favour my righteous cause; and let them say continually, "Let the Lord be magnified, who has pleasure in the prosperity of His servant."

PSALMS 35:27

The blessing of the Lord makes one rich and adds no sorrow with it.

PROVERBS 10:22

The Lord will send rain at the proper time from his rich treasury in the heavens and will bless all the work you do. You will lend to many nations, but you will never need to borrow from them.

DEUTERONOMY 28:12

Prayers

1. Thank you, Lord, that it is Your will, that I and my husband prosper and are in good health even as our minds prosper.35

2. I thank You that You have blessed us with all spiritual blessings in heavenly places, and by Your grace, Your blessing manifests into our finances.

3. Every curse and mindset of poverty, lack, and cycles of failure is broken over his life Jesus' name and by the blood of Jesus.

4. Let every poverty, defeatist, limiting and lack mindsets in him be replaced with the mindset of abundance, provision, faith, growth, generosity, drive and wealth.

5. Deliver him from every character trait and lifestyle that attracts poverty, such as sin, sexual promiscuity, pornography, indiscipline and lack of self-control, stinginess, laziness, sluggishness, apathy, lethargy, mediocrity, gambling, addiction, and pride.

6. Endow him with power, wisdom and faith, ideas to create wealth.

7. Give him strategies, ideas, creativity, intelligence, wisdom, information, ingenuity, opportunities, profitable inventions, multiple streams of income, successful and lucrative businesses, high conversion rates, and productive staff and connections to help him achieve financial freedom.

8. Bless the work of his hands and help him work smart, make passive income, and multiple streams of profitable income so that he has more than enough to give to his family and those in need.

---

35 Bible, 3 John 1:2

9. Reveal to him secrets to generate wealth, inventions, products, and services that are in line with purpose and prosperity.

10. He is financially intelligent, and he possesses every character needed for generating wealth, including wisdom, diligence, creativity, hard work, smartness, efficiency, and productivity.

11. He is a generous and proud provider for his family and those in need without complaint, hustle or burnout or excessive working hours.

12. He is a good man that leaves a wealthy and good inheritance for me and his children and their children.

13. My husband possesses cutting-edge wisdom and knowledge on investments and wealth-generating opportunities even during a pandemic or economic depression.

14. Open the floodgates of heaven and let there be rain over his business, career, investments, and work.

15. Let there be upgrades on his connections, job, career, business, and investments.

16. Upgrade his mindset, connections, and relationships. Draw people with an abundance mindset into his sphere of influence and remove every negative influences.

17. Grant him favour and connection with people, teachers, coaches, partners, staff, clients, and customers who will propel him along greater heights of success, purpose, and prosperity.

18. Help him to commit his ways to You and to good counsel.

19. Direct his financial decisions and steer him away from ideas and projects that will waste time, effort, and money.

20. Restore him from a season of drought and loss. May he have 10 times more than what he lost.

21. Rebuke the devourer on his behalf. Rebuke every demons, spiritual, mental, behavioural, and other forces that lead to financial loss, stagnancy, and poverty, in Jesus' name.

22. Close off any holes in his financial pockets that are causing him to lose money through debts, business mistakes, excessive spending, foolish giving, theft, fraud, sickness, and rejection.

23. He will no longer lose money but will invest and grow his money wisely.

24. May he involve himself in projects and passions that will lead to profit, passive income, and wealth.

25. May he make money and do business in line with purpose, not instead of or at the expense of purpose and family.

26. Give him wisdom to balance his finances and make adequate time and investments for his faith, relationships, and purpose.

27. Give him a generous mind to give joyfully to his wife, family, church, charities, and causes aligned with purpose, kingdom, and generosity.

28. Lead him to create or participate in projects that empower others to generate wealth, especially the less privileged, the poor, widows, orphans, and youths.

Day 19

HIS LOVE CAPACITY

Husbands, love your wives, just as Christ also loved the church and gave Himself up for her.

- Ephesians 5:25

One of our most important needs as women is love. It is therefore, no wonder that God states that the primary role of the husband is to love his wife and give himself up for her. Many men enter relationships with the best intention in the world to love their wives, but inevitably, leave their women love-deprived and hurt because of limited capacity and empty love tanks.

There are three factors that limit a man's ability to love which you must pray about.

1. His Love Tank

To love effectively and steadfastly, a man's love tank must be full. There are multiple ways this can happen. However, the best and most reliable source of love comes from knowing and receiving God's love through a close relationship with God, worship, and Bible study. God is love. He is the author of love. Therefore, for men to love from a place of abundance, they need to be well connected to the author and source of love and life. He also needs to have self-love and a community of men and people who pour into him.

2.　Love leaks and blocks

Many men enter relationships full of romance and attraction for their wives, but after a while, their love goes cold. In many cases, love turns into hate and resentment. This is because of inbuilt leaks and blocks to love. With the best intentions in the world, the demands of marriage, relationships, and fatherhood are simply more than a man with many love blocks can afford. Love leaks and blocks come from the following situations men commonly face:

- Lack of a loving father or mother figure
- Lack of a good role model for love
- Childhood trauma
- Rejection
- Inferiority complex
- Post-Traumatic Stress Disorder
- Mental health problems
- Low self-esteem
- Hurt and bitterness
- Prideful ego
- Anger
- Laziness, lethargy, and other character flaws

3.　Knowledge and wisdom

The Bible commands husbands to love their wives according to knowledge,[36] meaning that a man must study his wife, and gain knowledge about love and marriage, and the best way to love his wife. Many men genuinely feel love towards their wives but have no idea of what love is let alone the right way to love her. Other men have a very warped perspective of love through culture, religion, or upbringing. A competent husband, however, takes time and humility to unlearn some things and gain knowledge and understanding of how to uniquely love his partner in the love language she understands.

---

[36] Bible, 1 Peter 3:7

4.   Time investment

Finally, irrespective of what one's love language is, love requires time investment. No matter how rich or spiritual a man is, if he doesn't know how to prioritise his time appropriately and make enough quality time for love, his ability to love will be greatly limited.

Whatever is limiting a man's love capacity, capacity can increase, leaks can be repaired, and he can transform from the most selfish, egocentric, narcissistic, good-for-nothing man, to the most loving man. Love can begin to flow once the blocks are removed.

Let us pray:

Scripture Recitation

Love is patient and kind. Love is not jealous or boastful or proud, or rude. It does not dishonour others; it does not demand its own way. It is not irritable, and it keeps no record of wrongs. It does not rejoice about injustice, but rejoices whenever the truth wins. Love bears all things, believes all things, hopes all things, endures all things. Love never fails.

1 CORINTHIANS 13:4-8

Husbands, love your wives, as Christ loved the church and gave himself up for her, that he might sanctify her, having cleansed her by the washing of water with the word, so that he might present the church to himself in splendour, without spot or wrinkle or any such thing, that she might be holy and without blemish. In the same way husbands should love their wives as their own bodies. He who loves his wife loves himself. For no one ever hated his own flesh, but nourishes and cherishes it, just as Christ does the church.

EPHESIANS 5:25-33

In the same way, you husbands must give honour to your wives. Treat your wife with understanding as you live together. She may be weaker than you are, but she is your equal partner in God's gift of new life. Treat her as you should so your prayers will not be hindered.

1 PETER 3:7

PRAYERS

1. Transform my husband, Lord, with Your love, light, forgiveness, and kindness. May he know, connect, and experience Your love for him in all its dimensions and expressions.

2. May Your love drive out all fear from his life, including fear of hurt, rejection, and marriage.

3. Heal him from the feelings of not being loved, worthy, or enough.

4. Heal him from loneliness, rejection, guilt, and shame.

5. Give him the confidence to love himself, his wife, and others.

6. May he know that he is forgiven, and his sins and faults have been completely wiped away and forgiven by Jesus Christ.

7. Since he is forgiven, help him to easily let go of unforgiveness, grudges, bitterness, and offences from childhood, past and present experiences.

8. He is continually healed and filled with love and light so that he doesn't feel tired of doing good and showing love sufficiently.

9. In turn, I [his wife] will always honour, encourage, and appreciate his love and not take it for granted.

10. Strengthen him and may he never get weary of love.

11. Heal him Lord and deliver him from the following love blocks and leaks:

    o Lack of a loving father or mother figure
    o Lack of a loving husband role model
    o Childhood trauma or multiple childhood traumatic experiences
    o Failed relationship or marriage

- o Divorce
- o Rejection
- o Inferiority complex
- o Post-Traumatic Stress Disorder
- o Mental health problems
- o Low self-esteem.

12. Deliver him from all character traits that block love from his life. May he walk in the grace, wisdom, strength, and humility to let go of all character flaws that make it hard to love [mention those you are aware of]:

- o Hurt and bitterness
- o Stubbornness
- o Prideful ego
- o Anger issues
- o Laziness and lethargy
- o Impatience or low tolerance
- o Selfishness
- o Unforgiveness

13. It is his joy and pride to love me and make his family happy.

14. He finds joy, ease, and purpose in loving me and his children.

15. He is the best at loving me.

16. He is affectionate and speaks all my love languages including quality time, acts of service, gifts, physical touch and affection, affirmation.

17. He is thoughtful, effortful and creative in the way he expresses his love for me and our family

18. He is a great role model as a loving husband, and I am his number one admirer, fan and encourager.

19. He leads in love and is admired by family, friends, men, and young people.

20. Give him exceptional knowledge, grace, insight and understanding in:

- o The love of God
- o Love for his wife and children
- o Quality time
- o Affirmation and encouragement
- o Healthy pursuits
- o Thoughtful and creative gifts and dates
- o Acts of service
- o Affection
- o Physical touch

21. May he be rewarded richly for his labour of love in honour, wealth, health, purpose, fulfilment, influence, and more.

Day 20

PRAY AGAINST KING KILLERS

Do not give your strength to women, your ways to those who destroy kings.

Proverbs 31:3

There are many things that can kill kings, but today, we will be focusing on women who destroy kings and marriages. Please note, while this chapter focuses on some women who men encounter, this is not an excuse to categorise all or most women negatively, or to take away responsibility from a man for his choices. This chapter should be taken in context with all other concepts discussed in this book.

We will be discussing and praying about three types of dangerous women who quality men often encounter—the adulterer, the narcissist, and the "pick-me" lady. The common trait these women use to lure men with, is seduction.

Seduction

Seduction gives a woman the ability to be irresistibly attractive. Her mere presence alone creates such sexual tension that a man loses his senses and succumbs to all her demands. The seducer knows how to arouse a man profusely. Her words are soothing, her eye contact penetrates his soul, her walk makes him weak, and he feels her touch deep inside. A woman (or in some cases, man) who uses her seductive power in a negative way, is often intentionally after kings to seduce them to bed and get them to do things that will cause them to lose their dignity as kings. The seducer's victims include both married and single men.

I received a preview of the seducer's ways through a very vivid dream the Lord gave me many years ago.

In my dream, a lady walked into church while the preacher was preaching. She began to prophesy (give a word from God). The church I saw was a small church that had been through a lot of challenges. They were somewhat weary, dejected, tired, and in need of encouragement. This prophecy couldn't have come at a better time. The woman started off very encouraging and said the right words that were so needed by this church. She accurately described what the pastor and the people were going through. I felt a great sense of upliftment, comfort, and hope from the audience as the woman spoke. She continued to speak as her hands began to slide slowly up the pastor's thighs. The pastor stopped the woman and shielded himself, but her words were so mesmerising. They all wanted to hear what she was saying just a bit longer. The pastor was distracted again by her words as her hands started touching him. By the time he realised it, her hands had already penetrated inside of him. He couldn't guard himself or pull her hands out, as the woman had already gone straight into and through him. She then drew out something from the man (which I understood to be his power) and immediately walked out of the church. It happened so quickly. This well-meaning faith leader, his leaders, and congregants now realised what had happened. It was too late! He was very disappointed that he would allow this to happen.

There are a few things that God brought to my attention when I woke up from the dream.

The man and his church represented men, or a group of people who were burnt out spiritually, emotionally, professionally and ministerially. The man in my dream was tired, weary, and vulnerable, a perfect scenario for an intruder to slip in. Also, the man was a good man who feared God and had no intention of cheating on his wife. However, the conditions were right, and his guard was down.

As I recalled the scene in the dream, I became aware that there was no prayer covering for this pastor who was vulnerable at this time. There was also a very strained relationship between him and his wife. The wife was not on good terms with her husband. She was frustrated with her husband because she felt he did not meet her expectations in marriage. As a result, she brought this man down with words and regularly nagged him.

I was led to read Proverbs 7 not consciously knowing what the scripture said, but it perfectly described the seductress, her targets, and tactics to bring down kings and great men. Read proverbs 7 to understand her ways but here is a snippet.

*"With much seductive speech she persuades him; with her smooth talk she compels him. All at once he follows her, as an ox goes to the slaughter, or as a stag is caught fast till an arrow pierces its liver; as a bird rushes into a snare; he does not know that it will cost him his life. And now, O sons, listen to me, let not your heart turn aside to her ways; do not stray into her paths, for many a victim has she laid low, and **all her slain are a mighty throng**."* Proverbs 7:21-26

The narcissist

The first type of seducer I want to discuss is the narcissist, also known as a Jezebel. This woman operates in the spirit of control and manipulation and completely emasculates her victims. She takes on the masculine role and turns her victims into her lap dog. The narcissist could be a girlfriend, spouse, mother, child, family member, or even a work colleague, boss, or someone in a position of authority.

There are levels to the narcissistic personality, ranging from someone displaying traits of manipulation, to full-blown witches (or mind controllers). The worst kind of controllers use spiritual powers and exert absolute control over a man's mind, and money. I have heard stories about men under complete control from their mothers, who will keep them single and break up their relationships. If a man is under the spell of a witch, there is almost nothing that can be done for this man, except for separation and prayers or a good church deliverance program.

The narcissist's personality traits are surprisingly very common in today's world. Many narcissistic traits are more prominent in some modern women. A woman who displays control, over-masculinity, or inappropriate rulership over a man, or people, possesses narcissistic traits, to varying degrees. (Of course, many men possess narcissistic traits too).

The 'pick me'

This sounds like a strange choice but is very relevant here as I have seen first-hand how a man can completely not function in his role, as a man and husband, because of this type of woman around him, either as a wife, a mother, or a mistress.

A 'pick me' is simply a woman with no boundaries or standards around a man. (In psychology, this type of woman is similar to an enabler who enables bad behaviour in a person such as narcissism, or addiction). She spoils a man, allows him to behave how he wants with no consequence for his bad behaviour. In her desperation for his approval, she even rewards him when he does wrong. She does this because of low self-worth or by being in a culture where men are viewed as the prize. She feels lucky to have a man in her life, no matter what he does. This type of woman will steal the king in a man for several reasons. Firstly, humans, especially men, are wired to develop character through pressure, discipline, and boundaries. Therefore, women who spoil men inappropriately can limit their greatness and character. Psychologists have shown that a child who grows up with a lack of discipline and boundaries suffers the same consequences as a child who has suffered abuse. In my view, this is even more so the case for the male child.

Secondly, men are wired to be great through the help of women— their mother or spouse. A woman with no standards or boundaries and an inability to encourage good male character while discouraging bad behaviour will relinquish a man's greatness.

These 'pick me' women are also the type of women who offer themselves very easily and readily to a married man who makes little or no effort in return for sexual favours. Some men, unfortunately, can't resist the temptation.

The Adulterer

Adulterers are women (or men) who intentionally and unintentionally target married men to seduce them to have sex or inappropriate emotional relationships. I have heard many men say that once they got married, their desirability to other women increased dramatically. A friend told me how he started receiving nude pictures from another friend the moment he got married.

Adultery has many negative physical and spiritual consequences on a man, his family, and children. Many homes and well-meaning men have been destroyed by infidelity.

A man must exercise self-control, and couples must intentionally put boundaries in place to safeguard their home from infidelity, king killers, and home wreckers.

Let us pray:

Scripture Recitation

Their instructions are a shining light; their correction can teach you how to live. It will keep you from the immoral woman, from the smooth tongue of a promiscuous woman. Do not desire her beauty in your heart, and do not let her capture you with her eyelashes; For the levy of the prostitute is poverty, and the adulteress preys upon your very life. Can a man embrace fire and his clothes not be burned?

Can a man walk on hot coals without his feet being scorched? So, is he who sleeps with another man's wife; no one who touches her will go unpunished.

PROVERBS 6: 23-29

Watch and pray so that you will not fall into temptation

MATTHEW 26:41

And lead us not into temptation but deliver us from evil

MATTHEW 6:13

Finally, receive your power from the Lord and from his mighty strength. 11 Put on all the armor that God supplies. In this way you can take a stand against the devil's strategies

EPHESIANS 6:10-11

Prayers

1. Lord please protect my man from the bait of the seducer

2. Forgive him where he has succumbed to the seducer's bait

3. Lead him not into temptation but deliver him from evil and the stronghold of the seducer—the adulterer, narcissist, and "pick me".

4. Loose him from the strongholds of Jezebel in his family, work, and relationships.

5. Strengthen him and clothe him with Your armour of protection so that he can overcome the tricks and temptations of seducers.

6. Grant him self-discipline and, like Joseph, cause him to flee fast from temptation.

7. Give him discernment and open his eyes to recognise the seducer, even from a million miles away.

8. Let him recognise and be repulsed by seducers and king killers

9. Heal him and restore every lost virtue, strength, or power , character, resources, healthy relationships, positions and authority through past dealings with a seductive narcissist, 'pickme' or adulterer or any other king killers

10. Give him wisdom to know how to deal and set boundaries with controlling and manipulative people in his family, at work, and in relationships.

11. Help him to learn from past mistakes. He will not repeat past mistakes but will use the lessons for good.

12. May he be delivered from every negative effect of indiscipline and lack of boundaries in his upbringing and relationships.

Day 21

UPGRADE HIS RELATIONSHIPS

Your builders make haste; your destroyers and those who laid you waste go out from you.

- Isaiah 49:17

Show me your friends and I will show you who you are.

A man's friendships and relationships are one of the single most important factors that affect his destiny and could be the reason why he elevates or stagnates in life and marriage.

Separation comes before elevation. If you want to elevate your life and marriage, you must consider yours and your spouse's relationships. Relationships with people of higher calibres will help him elevate. Similarly, close relationships with people of lower calibre will bring him down. Hence, as a man elevates, his close friends need to elevate with him or separate, otherwise, they will slow him down with jealousy, dishonour, negative vibes, bad advice or influence.

Your man needs friends who will introduce him to his next level in masculinity, marriage, business, career, and purpose, physically, mentally and spiritually. He needs friends and mentors who will counsel and encourage him as he fights the battles of life and marriage.

As your man elevates to be a better man, from single to married, struggling to thriving, feminine to masculine, he will need a circle of friends and relationships to propel his elevation while losing friends who will hinder his growth.

Relationships can make or break a marriage relationship and affect the way a man thinks, so you must not fail to pray over your man's friendships, relationships, family, and spheres of influence.

Let us pray:

Scripture Recitation

Where no counsel is, the people fall: but in the multitude of counsellors there is safety.

PROVERBS 11:14

One who has unreliable friends soon comes to ruin, but there is a friend who sticks closer than a brother.

PROVERBS 18:24

Do not be misled: Bad company corrupts good character.

1 CORINTHIANS 15:33

Your builders hurry; Your destroyers and devastators Will go away from you.

ISAIAH 49:17

Prayers

1. Lord, I commit my husband's friendships and relationships into Your hands. May he have a close friendship with his Maker.

2. Let there be amicable and natural separation between him and his friends and family who are not good for his purpose and marriage.

3. Connect him with his purpose friendships, destiny helpers, connectors, and promoters, people who will connect, recommend, and introduce him to his next level in purpose, marriage, and business.

4. Connect him with purpose builders, leaders, helpers, mentors, counsellors, role models, and people who will give him sound advice, winning ideas, and solutions that will challenge him to be better in his masculinity, marriage, spirituality, finances, and health.

5. Connect him with his helpers, encouragers, cheerleaders, supporters, and promoters, who will encourage and cheer him when the battle of life gets tiresome.

6. Connect him with healthy mediators, counsellors, and advisers who will help him be a loving and competent husband and father.

7. Connect him with advocates who will fight for him and make it their personal mission to see him win in love, spirituality, business and life.

8. Connect him with staff members, mentees, and clients who he will impact greatly and who will serve his purpose.

9. Bless my in-laws and may their relationship with him and me be for the good of our marriage and purpose

10. Give him wisdom to recognise and detach from Judases, traitors, and friendly enemies whose purpose is to use, abuse, and betray him, cause division and sabotage his marriage.

Day 22

BREAK CURSES AND PROPAGATE

BLESSINGS

I will bless You and make Your name great. Blessed is he that blesses You and cursed is he that curses You.

- Genesis 12:3

Blessing is defined as the act of "invoking God's favour upon a person." As you pray, you are invoking God's favour and blessings on your husbands. When you bless your man, you must do so holistically, that is, spiritually, physically, and mentally.

A man may be physically fit, exercise daily, have muscles that make women look twice but he may be an absolute skeleton— good for nothing—in every other area of life. Similarly, a man may be rich and shower his wife and kids with every material wealth, but leave them starving of his time, respect, and love. In no time, his good looks or wealth becomes meaningless because he isn't holistically blessed in every area of his manhood—his spirit, soul, and body.

Spiritual blessings

One most important area of a man's life that is most ignored is his spirit man. You must always speak life and blessing into yours and your man's spirit. Firstly, because a man's spirit is the core of who he is and affects all other aspects of his life. Secondly, a man needs to be spiritually fit to protect his wife and household against spiritual attacks that may arise in the marriage. These attacks include sicknesses, spiritual attacks, and relationship challenges.

I have come to learn through several people I encountered recently that there are many good men out there who, if they were in Christ or spiritually robust, could have made awesome husbands for God's daughters. Please note, I am not generalising or saying that only spiritual people can enjoy a happy marriage or that Christians don't experience marriage breakdown. However, I am referring to a specific group of men who have given up on relationships and marriage altogether because of failed relationships. They lack the spiritual vigour required to heal and bounce back from traumatic experiences. After they had been battered through life, their source of strength and hope to break cycles of failed relationships and disappointment comes from their spiritual muscles. However, many men are very weak spiritually. I heard in my spirit as I encountered some of these men that "there is a population of men, until they connect with Christ, they will not enter a successful marriage." For these specific men, the power they need to fight and overcome generation cycles, childhood issues, character flaws, addictions, negative mindsets, failed relationships, abuse, and other issues can only come from Jesus Christ. We must therefore pray that these men come into an encounter with God's strength, healing, and revival.

Breaking curses and resetting generational legacies

Generational curses are negative patterns that occur across generations. If you experience certain cycles or patterns in your life, and notice the same patterns among your siblings, parents and grandparents, most likely there are generational curses at play in your bloodline which need to be dealt with.

The earliest account of this can be found in Genesis, the first book of the Bible. Three generations—Abraham and Sarah, their children, Isaac and Esau, their grandchildren Jacob and Rebecca, and their great-grandchildren—experienced the same patterns of barrenness, family discord, and other issues. I speak more about generational legacy and curses and the scientific and psychological evidence backing it in the Children's chapter. Whether you believe curses are real or not, they may be at play in your or your spouse's life. Particularly if there are recurring negative patterns in your life that don't seem to go away, it is worth praying and taking actions to interrupt the patterns.

The good news is that God has given you spiritual, psychological, and practical tools to interrupt negative patterns, reverse every curse in your life and replace them with God's blessings, and set new legacies for the next generation. Personally, studying, understanding, doing, and praying God's word has made an indescribable difference to my life and helped me break free from stubborn patterns in my life.

We are told that when Isaac prayed for his wife, the curse of barrenness was broken. As you pray for yourself and your spouse, may every curse and negative generational pattern be broken, in Jesus' name. May generational blessings and legacy of abundance, wealth, happy marriages, and relationships be our men's portions, in Jesus' name. May God give them direction and strength to take practical steps spiritually, mentally and physically to break generation curses, enjoy blessings and set new legacy for this and the next generation.

Let us pray:

Scripture Recitation

But Christ has rescued us from the curse pronounced by the law. When He was hung on the cross, He took upon Himself the curse for our wrongdoing. For it is written in the Scriptures, "Cursed is everyone who is hung on a tree". Through Christ Jesus, God has blessed the Gentiles with the same blessing He promised to Abraham, so that we who are believers might receive the promised Holy Spirit through faith.

GALATIANS 3:13-14

And I will make you a great nation, And I will bless you [abundantly], And make your name great (exalted, distinguished); And you shall be a blessing [a source of great good to others];. Blessed is he that blesses You and cursed is he that curses You. And in you shall all the families of the earth shall be blessed

GENESIS 12:3

Listen, I received a command to bless; God has blessed, and I cannot reverse it!

NUMBERS 23:20

Prayers

1. Thank you, that my husband is blessed with all spiritual blessings in the heavenly, psychological, and physical realms, in Jesus' name.

2. Thank you, Lord, that through the death of Jesus, all curses are broken for those who believe, and through Jesus Christ, he has access to God and the blessings of God.

3. I thank You that he is blessed spiritually and grows in his knowledge and awareness of spiritual and godly truths.

4. May he have a special encounter with his Creator and grow in the knowledge of who Jesus Christ really is and His unconditional love for mankind.

5. May he hear God more clearly, obey Him fully and live out God's purpose for his life.

6. Strengthen him in his inner man, spiritually and mentally.

7. Invoke in him a desire to pray and seek God and His truth, and direct him as he does so.

8. God's blessings are activated over his life, and he is free from any issues that have been passed down generationally in his life.

9. Lord, break the patterns and cycles of [state the patterns that apply]:

   o Limiting thinking and belief systems [specify the ones you are aware of, e.g. victimhood]
   o Stagnancy and hardship
   o Unforgiveness
   o Singleness
   o Loss
   o Broken relationships and divorce
   o Family feuds and fighting
   o Infidelity or sexual immorality

- Rejection and hatred from loved ones
- Poverty and financial hardship
- Barrenness

10. Lead, guide, and help him to take necessary practical steps, such as healing, counselling, self-development, or others, to break all negative generational cycles and reset new positive generational legacies.

11. Lord, rebuke all blessing thieves, or devourers from his life:
    - Divorce and failed relationships
    - Barrenness
    - Suicide
    - Alcoholism
    - Low self-esteem
    - Prideful ego
    - Poverty
    - Cycles of failure
    - Stagnated progress
    - Abuse
    - Anger and other character flaws
    - Crime

12. I thank You that my husband is blessed, fruitful, and productive.

Day 23

JOURNAL AND PERSONAL NOTES FOR

YOUR HUSBAND

Which of the themes discussed from the last 10 days resonates most with you regarding your desires for your husband?

What is the Lord telling you to do or what actions will you take to meet your desires mentioned above? [list actions and put realistic dates by which you will do]

SECTION 3

PRAYERS FOR YOUR CHILDREN AND GENERATIONAL LEGACY

Day 24

GENERATIONAL LEGACY—

PROPAGATE BLESSINGS AND BREAK CURSES ACROSS GENERATIONS

One generation shall commend your works to another and shall declare your mighty acts.

- Psalm 145.4

A generational legacy is a set of values, beliefs, behaviours, and outcomes that are passed down through a generational lineage. Legacies can be positive, negative or a mixture of both. It is commonly referred to as a generational blessing when legacies are positive or a generational curse when it is negative.

A fact of life most of us may not be aware of is the fact that events, patterns, thoughts, and behaviours we adopt and experience have commonly been pre-programmed through our family legacy and the actions of our parents and their parents. In fact, many children and adults are living out the consequences of actions carried out by their parents, their parents' parents and ancestors who lived before they were born.

The good news is that we as parents and influencers of children are in a powerful position to perpetuate new positive cycles, intercept negative cycles and instill new legacies for the next generation and the next.

This concept of generational legacies—blessings and curses are a phenomena acknowledged in the Bible and among spiritual people, but also within the secular and scientific world. Many lessons can be taken from the Bible as well as from neuro-science about the existence of generational legacies, and how to break generational curses and propagate generational blessings.

Dr Caroline Leaf, a neuroscientist, confirms this concept of generational legacies, stating that epigenetics, the signals, thought patterns, and behaviours that affect our genes, can be passed from generation to generation, meaning that an event that happened to a person can affect the genes of their children. This is also the same concept in intergenerational trauma where a person's trauma and its effects, are passed on through generations. For example, post-slavery syndrome describes the phenomena where a slavery mentality and its effect are still experienced generations down the line, even though slavery is no longer in existence in most parts of the world.

So why is it important to understand generational legacies, curses, and blessings?

Is it so that we devoid ourselves of responsibility for our own actions and blame them on our ancestors? Or is it so that we are left hopeless and have an apathetic mindset of, "Que, sera sera, whatever will be will be?"

Absolutely not.

Firstly, it is important to understand that as parents, teachers, or influencers we need to be aware that our behaviours not only affect us but more so, our children and generations after them. We, therefore, need to take responsibility for and be intentional about leaving good legacies and inheritances for our children.

Secondly, knowing the source of an issue enables us to resolve it accordingly. For example, the doctor who enquires about what illnesses run in your family during a medical examination uses that information to carry out specific tests and to advise you to be aware, vigilant, proactive, intentional, and adopt certain lifestyles that prevent certain ailments. In the same way, Dr Leaf writes that even though epigenetics is passed on generationally, a person can actively work on their thought patterns to change their own genetics. So, if you are aware of certain patterns in your family, you must not despise or blame your parents for your demise but take responsibility to break the cycle and create new cycles and legacies for yourself, your children, and generations unborn.

How To Reset Negative Generational Legacy

All concepts spoken about throughout this book are about how to break generational curses that are commonly experienced in marriages and families, and how to set new legacies for yourself, your spouse, and your children. Legacies are set and reset at three levels—spiritually, mentally, and physically. Therefore, actions that effectively reset and instill generational legacies need to affect all three dimensions.

Here are a few steps to consider:

1. Intentionally define a purpose, vision, or legacy for your family.

2. Take note of what legacies, belief or value systems, patterns, and cycles, both positive and negative, you and your spouse have inherited.

3. Create a plan on what changes you and your spouse need to make to become role models for your children, propagate your desired legacies and eliminate negative legacies.

4. Decide on what modes and ways you will use to leave desired legacies.

5. Begin to speak blessings over your family and children. All chapters in this book, especially section 3, contain blessings you can speak over your children that will change their lives and affect your legacy across generations.

6. Use Prayers and spiritual tools such as scriptures, the name and blood of Jesus, and Prayers in this book to break generational curses and speak blessings over your family.

7. Trust God as you pray for His help and commit your legacies to Him and listen to His instructions, and take action.

8. Remember Prayers without the required corresponding action is a waste of time.

Let us pray:

Scripture Recitation

Joseph is a fruitful bough, a fruitful bough by a spring; his branches run over the wall.

The archers bitterly attacked him, shot at him, and harassed him severely, yet his bow remained unmoved; his arms were made agile by the hands of the Mighty One of Jacob, by the God of your father who will help you, by the Almighty who will bless you with blessings of heaven above, blessings of the deep that crouches beneath, blessings of the breasts and of the womb. The blessings of your father are mighty beyond the blessings of my parents, up to the bounties of the everlasting hills. May they be on the head of Joseph, and on the brow of him who was set apart from his brothers.

GENESIS 49:22,26

You will be blessed in the city and blessed in the country. The fruit of your womb will be blessed, and the crops of your land and the young of your livestock—the calves of your herds and the lambs of your flocks. Your basket and your kneading trough will be blessed. You will be blessed when you come in and blessed when you go out.

The Lord will grant that the enemies who rise up against you will be defeated before you. They will come at you from one direction but flee from you in seven. The Lord will send a blessing on your barns and on everything you put your hand to. The Lord your God will bless you in the land he is giving you. The Lord will establish you as his holy people, as he promised you on oath, if you keep the commands of the Lord your God and walk in obedience to him. Then all the peoples on earth will see that you are called by the name of the Lord, and they will fear you. The Lord will grant you abundant prosperity.—in the land he swore to your ancestors to give you. The Lord will open the heavens, the storehouse of his bounty, to send rain on your land in season and to bless all the work of your hands. You will lend to many nations but will borrow from none.

DEUTERONOMY 14:3-13

Prayers

1. Thank you, Lord, that my children are blessed because You have blessed them.

2. May the strength, anointing, and help from God be upon my children [call them by name].

3. May they operate under open heavens. Open up the storehouse of blessings and wisdom over them.

4. The blessings of Jesus Christ rest upon the heads of my children.

5. Let them be fruitful and produce excellent outcomes in every good endeavour.

6. They are blessed relationally. They will grow, be fruitful, and successful spiritually in their relationship with God.

7. They also attract good, loving, and purposeful relationships and helpers for their lives, work, studies, destiny, and purpose—people who will be eager to help them achieve success.

8. My children are blessed and fruitful, biologically. Their children and children's children are blessed.

9. They are blessed mentally. Their minds give birth to winning ideas and solutions that will meet needs locally, nationally, and internationally.

10. Their thought patterns will align with wisdom, solutions, creativity, joy, and happiness.

11. They will bring joy, laughter, and happiness everywhere they go.

12. They are blessed academically—they will be the best among their peers and have wisdom better than their teachers.

13. They are blessed in their character. Help them to grow in the fruits of the spirit—love, joy, peace, patience, kindness, goodness, gentleness, and self-control.

14. May they grow in love and take actions of love and kindness that will be an example for their world to look up to.

15. May they exercise discipline, self-control, and time management with ease and speed.

16. May they overcome any challenge or suffering that life presents and may they come out of it stronger, better, and untouched.

17. By the blood of Jesus, break the following cycles and patterns. It will not be part of my children's struggle [list specific negative trends or patterns that are in your or family's lives]:

    o Sexual immorality and promiscuity

    o Indiscipline and procrastination

    o Lateness and delay

    o Sickness

    o Obesity

    o Mental health problems

    o Failed and difficult relationships

    o Academic struggle

    o Failure

    o Barrenness

    o Dishonour

Day 25

CHILDHOOD FOUNDATIONS

Train a child in the way he should go, and even when he is old, he will not turn away from it.

- Proverbs 22:6

Childhood is a crucial period in a person's life that forms the foundation or trajectory for adulthood. The scripture in Proverbs tells us that children will not depart from the training they get in their childhood.

The cruciality of a person's childhood in determining their future is also confirmed by a plethora of scientific, child development, and brain research that shows that virtually all aspects of a person's life—health, finances, behaviour, mindset, ways of thinking, educational attainments, cognition, and relationships—are determined and shaped during early childhood. It is, therefore, vital that parents and caregivers are intentional about shaping a child's life while they are young to give that child the best chance at success in their adult life.

As David asked in his Psalms, "if the foundations be destroyed what can the righteous do?"

Almost suggesting that there is nothing that can be done once childhood foundations are destroyed but to build a good foundation in the first place or go back to tear down and repair the faulty foundations that occurred during childhood. To set good foundations in the first place is much easier to achieve than uprooting and replacing bad foundations. In many cases, it is nearly impossible to completely repair damage inflicted in childhood.

The devotions and prayers throughout this and succeeding sections will change your children's lives, help you repair broken foundations, lay good foundations, and consequently, leave a positive generational legacy.

Even if you don't have biological children, you can pray for your future children as an act of faith, or for your non-biological children- people you have influence over.

Childhood foundations

Here are five principles to consider, to lay good foundations for your children and give them the best possible outcome in life:

(1)   Love

It is not enough to feel "love" for your children. You are to practically love your children but also meet their emotional, spiritual, and physical needs, and speak their love language- that is love them in practical ways they interpret as love. The five love languages or actions that make people feel loved are quality time, gifts, touch, words of affirmation, and acts of service. You can demonstrate love to your children through all five love languages although each child will uniquely have a preference for particular love language(s) that make them feel loved.

In addition to practically loving your child, love must be modelled on 5 levels- love for God, self, your spouse (and/or the child's parent), your child and love for others. It's a common mistake for parents to love their children while dishonouring the child's parent without realising that dishonour, rejection or maltreatment of a child's parent has the same effect as if you were directly maltreating the child, irrespective of how loving you are to your child.

(2)   Discipline

Loving and balanced discipline and boundaries are important for setting good foundations. A famous quote about discipline comes from the Bible, "spare the rod and spoil the child." This doesn't mean you should beat a child with a literal rod but, rod is used as a metaphor for discipline. Famous and well-renowned psychologist, Alfred Adler, cites over-pampering, a form of indiscipline, as one of the childhood conditions that have negative effects in adulthood. The other two he mentioned were physical ailment and neglect or abuse. In other words, indiscipline has the same negative impact on your child as abuse does.

(3)   Character

Children are like sponges. They soak in whatever they see and hear. Thus, you have the superpower to mould your children's characters through your own behaviour and what you teach and expose to them.

The best character traits to teach and model for your children are the fruits of God's spirit—love, joy, peace, patience, kindness, goodness, gentleness, discipline, faithfulness, and integrity.[37] It is also helpful to introduce them to historical figures or superheroes who exhibit these characters. For example, the life of Jesus and some Bible heroes are very good examples that children really enjoy learning about. These hero stories are taught in Sunday schools, faith schools or some cartoon or TV programs.

(4)   Success and wealth

One of the areas commonly overlooked but is so important to model and teach your children is, success. Competent parents intentionally set their children up for success. This means helping your children to be the best at what they have been called to be. Success, disciplines, wisdom, creativity, business, entrepreneurship, and financial literacy are all important values to start instilling in your children early on.

Robert Kiyosaki in his best-selling book, "Rich Dad Poor Dad," demonstrates how parenting can greatly impact a child's financial outcome. He lays out parenting principles commonly adapted by people with a wealth mindset and how these can set a child up for financial independence in adulthood.

(5)   Fear of God

Fear of God means honouring and reverencing God. There is nothing greater than teaching your children that they have a Creator who is not removed from their affairs. This God desires to be involved in our affairs, and all of

---

[37] Bible, Galatians 5:22

mankind will be accountable to the Creator for how they used God's gifts—the gift of life, health, wealth, family, and children—to fulfil his purpose in our lives and bring God glory.

If you believe there is a God, I encourage you to teach your children the ways of God, and how to reverence Him and to build a direct relationship with the Lord. I think it's important that children learn how not to worship self but to know that they have been intentionally created for a purpose by God. Children should be taught to live in gratitude and humility to the Creator of the universe.

Additionally, all parents should be aware of common parenting practices that are detrimental to children and their future. Scripture states "do not provoke your child to anger," which implies that parents can cause anger issues in children.[38]

3 common parenting practices that ruin children's future are

(1) Words. Death and life are literally in the tongue, as the Bible says. Hurtful, careless, and critical words can diminish your child's self-esteem. Low self-esteem can, in turn, negatively affect your child's future, including their performance, relationships, and parenting, thereby perpetuating the cycle of negativity and failed marriages through generations.

(2)Neglect. Failing to provide children with care, attention, and quality time, which are all basic needs of your children, are very common forms of abuse today. Many parents are too busy to spend quality time or to be affectionate with their children. This is a form of abuse.

(3)Favouritism. Favouring one or more children over others and comparing them has a negative impact on a child's self-esteem and can instill jealousy and division among siblings.

None of us are or will be perfect parents. Even the best parents on earth have limits and shortcomings. Where you, as a parent, have and will inevitably fail due to your own voids, negative childhood experiences, and trauma, God is able to fill those gaps.

---

[38] Bible, Ephesian 6:4

Furthermore, there is nothing greater than giving your children access to the best parent in the world through teaching them to have a direct relationship with God and His Word.

God certainly can help and parent your child where you fall short. I, and many others who have had very difficult childhoods but were saved through our relationship with God, are a living testament of the need for God's parenting. For some of us, God's parenting and presence in our lives has been a lifeline!

Pray today for God to help fill the gaps where you fall short.

Let us pray:

Scripture Recitation

Fathers, do not provoke your children to anger, but bring them up in the discipline and instruction of the Lord.

EPHESIANS 6:4

For I have chosen him so that he will command his children and his house after him to keep the way of the Lord by doing what is right and just. This is how the Lord will fulfil to Abraham what He promised him.

GENESIS 18:19

Discipline your children, and they will give you peace; they will bring you the delights you desire.

PROVERBS 29:17

My grace is sufficient my strength is made perfect in your weakness....so that the power of God will rest on you.

2 CORINTHIANS 12:9

Prayers

1. Lord, I pray for Your mercy and forgiveness in any way I have not trained my child in the right way, knowingly or unknowingly.

2. Let my eyes and consciousness become open to any flaws in the way I bring up my child.

3. I receive wisdom, grace, and the ability to be the best parent for my child and give them the best training and foundation for their future.

4. Please give me the spirit, character, wisdom, knowledge, understanding, counsel, and strength I need to be the best parent for my children.

5. I receive wisdom to solve and overcome any challenges that may arise in my parenting. Help me handle every situation with my child in wisdom.

6. I am a great love role model for my children.

7. I model good character—love, joy, peace, patience, goodness, gentleness, self-control, and discipline, both in the ways I relate to myself, my children, my spouse, their parents, and others.

8. Help me to discipline and influence my children effectively and healthily in love, not excessively, ineffectively or in a way that will provoke them to anger.

9. Lord, forgive me and I repent of any hurtful words that I may have spoken to my children.

10. Help me speak words that will be nourishing to their souls, healthy to their bodies, and uplifting for their spirits.

11. I speak words of encouragement that will build my children, not words that will tear them down.

12. I speak wise words that instill wisdom in my children, bring solutions to their challenges, and corrections to their errors.

13. I bring up my child in the path of success and purpose, spiritually, morally, intellectually, educationally, financially, creatively, and otherwise.

14. Help me, Lord, not to provoke my child to anger. Where I have done so in the past, help me to speak and do things that will bring healing and reconciliation to my child.

15. Their influencers—family, grandparents, teachers, nannies—are people who also model God's love to them.

16. Expose and separate my children from anyone who will have a negative influence over their formative years.

17. Heal any brokenness in my child's upbringing during their formative years and help me to repair any damages done.

18. Lord, please fill any parental gaps or voids in my child.

19. Lord, bring my child up and send father and mother figures, nurturers, mentors, coaches, teachers, spiritual leaders, and shepherds their way who will care for them like their own child (particularly if one or both of their parents is absent).

20. Help me bring my child up in the ways of the Lord.

Day 26

YOUR CHILDREN'S DESTINY

—DESTINY HELPERS AND KILLERS

And we know that God causes all things to work together for good to those who love God, to those who are called according to His purpose.

- Romans 8:28

Purpose is what a child has been called to do. Destiny is the various positions, places, and journeys at specific times the child is supposed to take along the path of fulfilling purpose.

If a child is destined for greatness and to do good, to influence and affect many people's lives for good, this becomes a threat to evil forces and their agenda to propagate evil and fight against what is good. This threat to evil forces is worse if the child is or will be a practicing Christian whose life will glorify Yahweh God. If you go through a lot of opposition or complications during pregnancy or huge pressure to abort or terminate your child, it is usually the case that you are about to give birth to a special child destined for greatness and God's purpose.

This was the case with Moses. Moses' destiny was to free the Israelites out of slavery. However, during the time of his birth, a decree had gone that all the male children should be killed. This also happened to Jesus. As soon as Jesus' star was located, and it was noted that he had a bright future to be king and to save the world from sin, the king at the time, Herod, became threatened and made a decree that all the young male boys should be killed.

Every great child has a star that is visible to spiritual beings. A child with a bright and great star will be fought with sickness, depression, or one issue or the other before or after birth and especially during their childhood years. The plan is to either kill or frustrate the child early, to ensure that he or she does not fulfil their purpose. You, however, can win this fight with God's help, Prayers, and words of blessing over your child.

There are three significant factors that affect your child's purpose and destiny:

1.   Destiny helpers. These helpers include friends, nannies, teachers, role models, mentors, and influencers who will guide your children along the right path and facilitate their destiny and purpose. In today's world, children are influenced largely outside the home—they may be well brought up by their parents but can fall into the wrong influence outside of the home, which can corrupt a child's good upbringing. As the Bible saying goes, "Evil company corrupts good manners."[39].

2.   Destiny killers are spiritual, psychological, and physical factors that can kill, steal, or destroy the lives and destinies of your children. Herod was a ruler who famously came against many of God's great children in the Bible with the intention to stop God's plans through their lives. Herod attempted to assassinate Jesus, beheaded John, and imprisoned Peter. Likewise, there are spiritual Herod at work today whose purpose is to antagonise God's children, to kill and imprison them so that God's purpose for their lives isn't fulfilled.

3.   Destiny delayers or derailers. If the enemy fails to kill your child or their destinies, he often delays or derails them from aligning with destiny. It is important we pray against demonic delays in the lives of our children so that they will operate in God's timing and seasons for their lives. They will not be derailed or delayed in Jesus' name!

Let us pray:

---

[39] Bible, 1 Corinthians 15:33

Scripture Recitation

The thief's purpose is to steal and kill and destroy. My purpose is to give them a rich and satisfying life.

JOHN 10:10

For it is God who is at work in you, both to will and to work for His good pleasure.

PHILIPPIANS 2:13

The Lord will fulfill his purpose for me; your steadfast love, O Lord, endures forever. Do not forsake the work of your hands.

PSALM 138:8

The LORD frustrates the plans of the nations; He thwarts the devices of the peoples   but *the counsel of the LORD stands forever, the plans of his heart to all generations.*

PSALMS 33:10-11

Many are the plans in the mind of a man, but it is the purpose of the LORD that will stand

PROVERBS. 19:21

Devise a plan, but it will be thwarted; state a proposal, but it will not happen. For God is with us

ISAIAH 8:10

Those who will rebuild you are coming soon, and those who destroyed you will leave.

ISAIAH 49:17

Prayers

1. Thank you, Lord, for Your promises and blessings over my children.

2. Lord, I commit my children into Your hands. Guide them along the right path of purpose, destiny, and greatness.

3. They are who God says they are and who God has called them to be.

4. They are light in this world that shines in the darkness.

5. They have a positive influence over their peers and beyond.

6. They are strong enough to resist any negative influences over their lives but instead influence others for the better.

7. I pray against the spirit of Herod, in Jesus' name—the one who comes to kill kings, queens, and leaders for the sake of their destiny.

8. Abort his plot to divert my children from their destiny through untimely death, sickness, bullying, imprisonment, wrong associations, discriminations, and deception.

9. I pray against all destiny derailers. Lord, deliver my children from all events that will derail or delay them from their God-ordained purpose.

   o Bad friends and influencers
   o Gangs
   o Rapists
   o Sickness
   o Death
   o Accidents
   o Addictions

10. Expose and separate my child from all destiny killers.

11. Stop all demonic delays and distracters, in Jesus' name.

12. My children are synchronised and syncopated to God's timing, purpose, plans, and will for their lives. They will do God's will in the correct time and season ordained for them, in Jesus' name.

13. I call forth and release my children's destiny helpers and purpose friendships, relationships, nannies, babysitters, teachers, mentors, counsellors, coaches, and influencers, who will guide and serve them along the path of destiny, purpose, and success.

14. I call forth all their helpers. May they favour and connect with my child through nursery, school, college, university business, summer school, internships, work, entrepreneurship, and ministry.

15. My children will find favour with their destiny helpers, and influential people will be attracted to my children to guide, teach, and serve their greatness.

16. Connect my children with quality friendships, exceptional mentors, coaches, advisors, leaders, and influencers who will take interest in, favour, invest in, and have a positive impact on their lives.

17. I pray against any plan of the forces of darkness to steal time, gifts, talents, joy, and happiness from our children.

18. My children will not die but live to declare the works and purpose of God.

19. All plans of the evil one to kill our children or their destiny is overturned; their hands will not perform their enterprise.

20. My children will not be victims of corruption, sexual immorality, rape, addiction, gang activity, kidnapping, occultism or violence.

21. Build a hedge of fire and protection around my children from evil ones.

22. Lord, deliver my children from any evil and temptations they find themselves in currently.

Day 27

EXCELLENCE

Then this Daniel was preferred above the presidents and princes because an excellent spirit was in him; and the king thought to set him over the whole realm.

- Daniel 6:3

Excellence is the quality of being outstanding or extremely good in one or more areas of life. An excellent child is a child who performs way beyond his or her age-group in talent, academic performance, creativity, or productivity. Examples include young entrepreneurs, child actors, mathematicians, or scientists.

Daniel and his friends, from a young age, had excellence which made them better than all their peers. We are told that their diet contributed to their excellence. They were very disciplined, ate a vegetarian diet, and did not consume—eat, watch, listen to, or indulge in—what their peers consumed. As the saying goes, "you are what you eat," meaning we are a product of the content we consume—food, words, music, visuals, and teachings.

Jeremiah was another Bible personality who stood out for his age. He had a special visitation from the Lord that helped him overcome the limitation and insecurity around his age so that he became the prophetic voice, influencer, and adviser of his day, even though he was young. Likewise, David, through his encounter with Samuel the prophet, was anointed and activated to be king. He won battles in his time that even the giants and gurus in his day didn't win.

When cultivating excellence in your children, it is important to think of factors that can cause children to operate in excellence. These include:

- A spirit and natural aptitude for excellence
- Supernatural encounter
- Discipline
- Gifts—talents and abilities given by God
- Healthy diets
- Good parenting
- Good family dynamics
- Early exposure to excellence through school, training, coaching or internships

It is important to emphasise that excellence does not exclude children with disabilities, including dyslexia, dyspraxia, autism, or any other types of disabilities or handicaps. I am encouraged by the scripture that says that God's grace is sufficient for us, and His power is made perfect and manifests through our weaknesses and infirmities. Scripture also tells us that God specialises in using weak people, and He demonstrates His power through people who may have been written off by society. There are many stories of people with serious ailments labelled as weak, low-achieving, disabled or any other negative labels but who go on to achieve greater things than their peers without any disabilities.

Nick Vujicic's story is very inspiring. He was born without hands or limbs but went on to not only do awesome things like drive and cook but has achieved beyond many abled-bodied people—he has written several bestselling books and gives motivational talks all around the world. All this to say, you must not allow any limitations to hinder your children from being excellent in this world. With God's grace and spirit of excellence, anything great is possible for your children, irrespective of their weaknesses, challenges, or disabilities.

Enemies of growth progress and excellence

There are factors that hinder your child's excellence and potential. I call them enemies of excellence. Many times, we see children who start out excellently.

Over time, or as they grow, they digress into mediocrity and backwardness because of enemies of excellence such as:

- Spiritual attacks
- Racism and discrimination
- Wrong associations—teachers or friends
- Indiscipline
- Sluggishness
- Distractions
- Addictions
- Depression and anxiety
- Dyslexia and other learning disabilities
- Memory loss
- Substance misuse
- Bad upbringing
- Trauma
- Abuse

It is important that, as parents, you are aware of and tackle the factors that hinder excellence and lead to mediocrity or cycles of failure and poor performance in your children.

Let us pray:

Scripture Recitation

I have heard that the spirit of the gods is in you, and that you have insight, intelligence, and extraordinary wisdom.

DANIEL 5:14

Whenever the king consulted them in any matter requiring wisdom and balanced judgement, he found them ten times more capable than any of the magicians and enchanters in his entire kingdom.

DANIEL 1:20

My grace is all you need. My power works best in weakness. So now I am glad to boast about my weaknesses, so that the power of Christ can work through me.

2 CORINTHIANS.12:9

The LORD will make you the head and not the tail; you will only move upward and never downward, if you hear and carefully follow the commandments of the LORD your God, which I am giving you today.

DEUTERONOMY 28:13

Prayers

1. Thank you, Lord, for blessing my child in every way, with talents, gifts, intelligence, and excellence in all matters of wisdom, knowledge, creativity, understanding, and expertise with excellence.

2. Release on my children a spirit and character of excellence, an ability to excel in their gifts, talents, and calling.

3. May my children have divine and prophetic encounters that will activate and revive God's call and gifts in their lives.

4. I pray for my child that they will possess all character traits that support excellence, including drive, motivation, and discipline.

5. Connect them early with people, associations, opportunities, schools, internships, and programs that will facilitate and nurture their excellence and greatness.

6. Perfect all their imperfections, including their character, lifestyle, academics, businesses, and relationships.

7. My children will be young entrepreneurs

8. They will excel in their academics and in all entrance exams.

9. They have wisdom greater than their teachers.

10. They are a positive example for their peers in character, speech, excellence, academics, business, creativity, art, and influence.

11. Give them positive influence and may all who encounter them be impacted to be happier and better.

12. Bless their creativity and use it for Your purpose and glory in their lives.

13. Through the name and blood of Jesus, I pray for deliverance of my child from enemies of excellence and progress.

14. Deliver and heal them from:

    o Spiritual attacks
    o Indiscipline
    o Sluggishness
    o Distractions
    o Addictions
    o Depression and anxiety
    o Dyslexia and other learning disabilities
    o Loss of memory
    o Substance misuse
    o Abuse

15. May their mind, body, and soul be washed clean by the blood of Jesus.

16. May they be healed and overcome all learning challenges.

17. Quicken their brain cells.

18. Remove every negative influence and character and confidence killers in the form of negative words, friends, teachers, families, TV, influencers, or media personalities.

19. Takeaway bad attitude, stubbornness, disobedience, and pride from my child.

20. My children will arise and shine.

21. Free them from all limitations, restrictions, impediments, imprisonments, and glass ceilings assigned to stall their God-given influence and excellence.

22. My children [call them by name] will not be censored, hindered, dishonoured, marginalised, cut-off, shut down, silenced, isolated, or bullied.Their God-given ideas, talents, gifts, voices, opinions, creativity, and solutions will prevail [repeat 3 times].

Day 28

POWER, POLICIES AND POLITICS OVER

YOUR CHILDREN

Pray for kings and others in power, so we may live quiet and peaceful lives as we worship and honour God.

- 1 Timothy. 2:1-2

Whilst parenting is the biggest influence over a child and their adulthood, politics and government powers through schools and culture is another huge influence on our children, since they spend most of their time in school and with their friends.

School is, therefore, a place where values, norms, and behaviours are propagated into society through children in early life, through the school curriculum and taught values.

Government and the powers that be in society are very aware of the importance of a child's formative years. The evidence base for influencing society or behaviours in a child's early years is huge, so early programming is a recognised effective strategy to implement agendas and behaviour change among a population. For example, the government in the UK now recognises the effectiveness of combatting society's ills such as obesity, heart disease, and substance misuse, by investing in health promotions and education in early years and in schools. This is positive.

On the contrary, government or non-governmental agencies can intentionally or unintentionally influence a child negatively through values, cultures and behaviours that are being propagated through the school curriculum, especially if they are directly opposed to Christian values. Some of these values include normalising abortion, atheism, sexual disinhibitions, gender mutilations, and others.

I wholeheartedly agree that our children must be taught to respect and tolerate people from all faiths, values, and sexual orientations. However, tolerance for one view should not come at the cost of tolerance for another religious view. We should be able to coexist, love, and respect each other, while being free to disagree. Our thoughts and opinions must not be controlled by government. My child should be free, like everyone else, to say, "I love you, but I and/or my faith do not agree with your lifestyle." Respect should work both ways!

Back when I was in school, school would present pros and cons of different political or religious matters, giving a child the opportunity to be critical and make their decision, rather than intentionally propagating anti-Christian values while shutting down Christian values and opinions. These days children are being penalised for holding or sharing their views on matters in line with their Christian faith. We hear more and more stories of children who have been punished and even excluded for expressing their religious beliefs about sex. This ought not be.

In light of this, we need to pray for our government and decision makers that they will be guided by godly values and morality, especially where children are concerned, while, of course, promoting love, tolerance, and respect for people from various religious and non-religious beliefs.

Discrimination in schools

Secondly, it is important to be aware of policies and practice in schools that discriminate against children because of their race, sex, disabilities, or religion. Conscious and unconscious biases in schools from teachers can play a role in limiting a child's performance and potential. For example, research such as the independent Timpson Review of school exclusion showed that institutional racism in schools results in discriminatory practices and shapes teachers' expectations of acceptable behaviour. The review showed that

Black Caribbean children are around 1.7 times more likely to be permanently excluded compared to White British children, and that the disproportionate exclusion of Black students came from labelling, stigmatisation, and problematic teacher assessments.

Relationships and bullying

Aside from policies and practice from school systems, relationships in school with pupils and teachers can affect a child's performance, their behaviour, and confidence. Favour, respect, and concern for children help them thrive. On the other hand, negative words, picking on, and bullying in schools not only affect children's mental wellbeing and confidence but also their school performance.

I pray that your children will find favour with their teachers and other pupils. People teachers, mentors, and peers will go above and beyond to support, help and favour your children. May God give the parents and teachers of any child connected to you that is going through bullying, and even your child, wisdom to overcome and turn that situation around for both your child and other children affected. Your child will be bold to stand up against bullies at school.

Family separations

Government agencies such as social services are crucial agencies to protect families and children and intervene when they are at risk. I believe most of the time these agencies do a great job in supporting and protecting vulnerable adults and children. However, there are many accounts where government agencies or social services have gotten involved in a family and unfairly separated and disrupted the family because of a number of reasons ranging from racism, false accusations, poor mental health of the parent, or domestic violence. For example, there is evidence that shows that social services are biased against families from certain ethnic backgrounds.

This is a topic dear to my heart as I had experienced this personally and also know of two mothers who were victims of abusive husbands. As a result, they got separated from their children. Instead of the mothers, who were also victims, getting support to heal and protect their children. One of the mothers became mentally unwell and does not know the whereabouts of her children to date. This ought not be. Let us pray:

Scripture Recitation

All your children shall be taught by the LORD, and great shall be the peace of your children.

ISAIAH 54:13

But seek the welfare of the city where I have sent you into exile, and pray to the Lord on its behalf, for in its welfare you will find your welfare.

JEREMIAH 29:7

The king's heart is a stream of water in the hand of the Lord; He turns it wherever He will.

PROVERBS 21:1

Now the LORD had caused the Egyptians to look favourably on the people of Israel. And Moses was considered a very great man in the land of Egypt, respected by Pharaoh's officials and the Egyptian people alike.

EXODUS 11.3

"Blessed be the name of God forever and ever, to whom belong wisdom and might. He changes times and seasons; He removes kings and sets up kings;

DANIEL 2:21

Devise a plan, but it will be thwarted; state a proposal, but it will not happen. For God is with us."

- ISAIAH 8:10

Prayers

1. I pray over our government and decision makers within the education system, social services and children's agencies. We pray for our policy makers, ministers for education, school governors, head teachers, teachers, and OFSTED officials. We pray for social services, their managers and workers. We pray for the legal systems, and the child protection unit, and every other child agency.

2. We pray that You bless them with wisdom, counsel, knowledge, and understanding, so that they will lead in godly wisdom and implement policies in the direction that is beneficial for our children and society.

3. Lord, put righteous people in strategic and influential positions, who will act and implement the best policies for children. Endow them with power and wisdom.

4. Remove all people who have a diabolic assignment to corrupt children and society and oppose Your people in power.

5. Let all policies, legislations, and action plans be in line with good, success, morality, righteousness, and godly values which will benefit our children.

6. Erase all negative agendas, policies, and strategies that are against godly values and that will corrupt our children and their morality and value system.

7. Lord, expose and highlight personnel, policies and practices that are a source of discrimination, racism, limitation, corruption, and ungodliness for our children. May they be overturned and replaced with godly ones.

8. Surround my children with Your cloak of favour. They will experience favour, special treatment, and kindness with their peers,

teachers, and headteachers who will provide all the help my child needs in school.

9. My child and their God-given values, ideas, talents, gifts, voices, opinions, creativity, and solutions will prevail.

10. They will not be censored, hindered, dishonoured, marginalised, cut off, shut down, silenced, isolated, or bullied.

11. All prejudice, discrimination, limitations, restrictions, imprisonments, and glass ceilings against my child are shattered, in Jesus' name.

12. My children will not be bullied. Instead, they will stand defiantly against bullying, and they will defend any child being bullied.

13. Execute Your righteousness and justice for any child or family being bullied or mistreated by people in positions of power—social services, schools, or others. Give students, teachers and headteachers wisdom on how to take effective action against bullying, in Jesus' name.

Day 29

FIGHTING FAMILY FEUDS

—SIBLINGS AND PARENTAL RIVALRY

How good and pleasant it is when brothers live together in unity! For harmony is as precious as the anointing oil that was poured over Aaron's head, that ran down his beard and onto the border of his robe … And there the LORD has pronounced His blessing, even life everlasting.

- Psalm 133:1-3

Rivalry during childhood, between parents, siblings, and children, are a source of bitterness and pain in a child's life. This bitterness becomes the foundation that attracts contentions, strife, and rejection that continues well into the child's adult years, affecting their lives and relationships negatively.

Bitterness is one of the most common keys that opens the doors to many demons and ailments in a person's life, including discord, hate, cycles of failed relationships, and sicknesses. Scientific research has also confirmed this link between bitterness and many physical ailments, including cancer.[40]

---

[40] Segrin, C., & Flora, J. (2017). *Family conflict is detrimental to physical and mental health.* In J. A. Samp (Ed.), *Communicating interpersonal conflict in close relationships: Contexts, challenges, and opportunities* (p. 207–224).

These are common sources of bitterness and strife in a child's life:

1. Parental conflict

Conflict between parents greatly impacts a child's wellbeing and future relationships. Children who witness conflict between their parents have poorer mental and physical health outcomes and can become suicidal in extreme cases. Several Youth and Adolescence studies found that children exposed to parental fighting and who grew up in high conflict homes are more likely to experience negative health and educational outcomes, including low self- esteem, increased heart rates, stress hormone responses, depression, anxiety, behavioural problems, disrupted brain development, and sleep disturbance. Living in a high-conflict family also affects school performance and increased the likelihood of dropping out and exclusions.

Conflict between parents can go on to affect the future of children's relationships as a child's attachment to their parents in early years is negatively impacted by parental conflict. This is known as insecure attachment, which, if not addressed, can be the cause of relationship problems. Not to mention several poor behaviour and communication patterns that are adopted by children from their parents and can go on to impact future relationships if these are not identified and unlearnt.

2. Sibling rivalry

Sibling rivalry refers to chaos, hatred and fighting between brothers and sisters in a household. While sibling quarrels are quite normal, sibling rivalry happens when sibling disputes escalate into hatred, excessive quarrelling, and betrayals between siblings. This rivalry is another common open gate for the demons of chaos and bitterness to enter into a person's life and impact the child's future relationships, leaving them in a perpetual cycle of singleness, divorced and unhealthy relationships. This is especially the case when rivalry between siblings continues to get worse and more serious with age, leading to rejection, hatred, and betrayal among family members.

There are two points I want to highlight relating to sibling rivalry. Firstly, many times sibling rivalry is hereditary and passes from generation to generation. If you, or someone you know, have experienced this kind of nasty divisions between siblings or family members, you will find that the same pattern is experienced in their parents' and grandparents' family. This was the case as far back as the time of Abraham, in1821 BC. Abraham experienced conflict with his nephew, Lot. His sons Isaac and Ishmael, also experienced conflict and had to part ways. Isaac's sons also did the same. They hated their brother Joseph so much that they plotted to kill him.

If you experienced excessive hatred and conflict with your siblings, and if your parents experienced the same thing, that conflict is likely a risk for your children, and you will need to be more intentional about fostering love between your children, both practically and spiritually.

Secondly, parents play a big role in propagating or eliminating rivalry between siblings through favouritism towards one or more of their children.

Jacob in the bible, preferred Joseph of all his sons and did not hide it, leading to envy and jealousy from his brothers. I know from personal experience that a parent's obvious show of favour and love, or even disdain for one of their children over the other is a major factor that leads to sibling rivalry, rejection, low self-esteem, and other mental health issues in the less preferred child. It may be natural for parents to prefer one child over another child, but parents must be aware of the consequences and make extra effort to either hide their preference or intentionally affirm the less preferred child. As far as I am concerned openly comparing children to one another is a form of abuse and is evil! Sadly, this is common.

3. Rivalry between parents and their children

Last, but certainly not least, the damage that comes from ongoing contentions between a father and his child, particularly sons, or a mother and her child can be very damaging. Parent-child feuds, especially if neglect, abandonment, and abuse are involved, have the most damaging impact on a child and lead to personal brokenness, anger, and mental health disorders. It also leads to the child experiencing broken relationships through to adulthood. Common causes of parent child rivalry or wounds include:

(1) **Neglect and abuse.** Parent often fail in their provision of love and care for their child, through verbal or physical abuse, rejection, and neglect. Neglect, the most common type of abuse, is when a parent fails to meet the physical, emotional, social, educational, and safety needs of a child, including

the child's need for quality time, affection, and words of affirmation. Over-criticism is also very detrimental to a child's life.

(2) **Abuse or neglect of the child's parent**. Many children resent one of their parents for the way they treated the other parent.

(3) When discipline goes wrong. This is both when a child is not disciplined, is mollycoddled, or over-disciplined. There is a thin line between discipline and abuse, and many parents, particularly from African heritage, often abuse their children, either physically and/or verbally, under the guise of discipline and culture. On the other hand, western or westernised parents tend to under-discipline or over-pamper their children. Over-pampering has the same impact on a child in adulthood as abuse. Hence, when disciplining your children, do so in love, ensuring that the line between discipline and abuse is not crossed.

Spiritual Origin and Resolution of Conflict

The spirit of God is a spirit of peace, love, joy, patience, kindness, goodness, gentleness, faithfulness, and self-control. So, for a family where there is much conflict, the first solution is to invite the spirit of God and the Prince of Peace, Jesus Christ, to rule in your heart and character, and in the heart of every member of your household.

Additionally, practical steps to resolve conflict must be taken, such as inviting a trained mediator or counsellor to help, or take courses around conflict management. However, it's worth noting that family feud originates from the spirit realm, from anti-relationship demons whose job is to create division, disputes and chaos, and ensure that the family unit is broken from generation to generation. Hatred and division within the family not only affect family relationships but also negatively impacts a person's relationship with God, giving the enemy of our soul further reason to attack God's children with conflict. Family members get distracted and expend energy fighting one another instead of fighting the true enemy—the devil and his demons. In today's prayer, welcome the spirit of peace to take the lead in your home, and pray spiritual warfare prayers that will drive out the demons of conflict from your homes. Pray for healing, forgiveness and reconciliation, and that the fires of fighting, rivalry and family feuds be quenched forever. Also, pray that God will lead you to seek effective practical help. Let us pray:

Scripture Recitation

He will restore the hearts of the fathers to their children and the hearts of the children to their fathers, so that I will not come and smite the land with a curse.

MALACHI 4:6

My people will abide in a peaceful habitation, in secure dwellings, and in quiet resting places.

ISAIAH 32:18

But the Holy Spirit produces this kind of fruit in our lives: love, joy, peace, patience, kindness, goodness, faithfulness.

GALATIANS.5:22

We know how dearly God loves us, because He has given us the Holy Spirit to fill our hearts with His love.

ROMANS 5:5

For where you have envy and selfish ambition, there you find disorder and every evil practice. But the wisdom from above is first pure. It is also peace-loving, gentle at all times, and willing to yield to others. It is full of mercy and the fruit of good deeds. It shows no favouritism and is always sincere.

JAMES 3:16-17

Prayers

1. Lord, forgive me in any way I have harboured hurt, pain and bitterness in my heart towards my own parents, siblings, family, or children, and thus, opened the door to conflict in my home.

2. Forgive my parents, grandparents, and fore parents, and family for sowing and nurturing the seed of division and rivalry in my family lineage.

3. Please search mine and my spouse's heart to see if there are any unforgiveness and bitterness there. Heal us, cleanse us, and deliver us.

4. I reject and renounce conflict, quarrelling, hatred, and bitterness from my heart and home.

5. I uproot the foundations of bitterness from its source, in Jesus' name.

6. All generational foundations and curses, familial spirits of dispute, and divisions attached to my family are destroyed by the blood of Jesus from the source, in Jesus' name.

7. We choose mercy, forgiveness, favour, love, kindness, and tolerance over hatred in my household.

8. Holy Spirit of God, Prince of Peace Jesus Christ and Father of love, Yahweh, I welcome You into my heart and home.

9. My home is a haven of peace, love, harmony, laughter, healing, and understanding.

10. Spirit of God, Your leadership, culture, righteousness, peace, and joy fill every room and heart in this home.

11. Spirit of God, reign in my home. Let Your character—love, joy, peace, patience, kindness, goodness, faithfulness, gentleness, and self-discipline—reign in my life, and between all members of my household, in Jesus' name.

12. Let all conflict, hurt and bitterness be resolved swiftly and replaced with forgiveness, reconciliation, and mercy.

13. Let there be immense peace, love, and understanding between me and my spouse (or my children's parent) and between all members of my household.

14. Help us apply wisdom to identify, correct, or cut off outsiders who knowingly or unknowingly create conflict within my family.

15. Give me and my spouse wisdom to resolve conflicts amicably, and may we be good examples of love and harmony for our children.

16. Let unity dwell in my home. May myself and my spouse, with God, be like a three-part cord that cannot be broken.

17. Let there be immense love, harmony, and peace between my children. They will cover, protect, and defend one another.

18. They will compete with one another on who loves the best.

19. Fill every member of this household with the spirit and wisdom of peace so that we will all apply and pursue peace, submission, and kindness with one another.

20. Thank you, Lord, that my home overflows with laughter, joy, celebrations, peace, healing, and fun, in Jesus' name. Amen.

Day 30

YOUR CHILDREN'S SALVATION

Choose today whom you will serve. Would you prefer the gods your ancestors served beyond the Euphrates? Or will it be the gods of the Amorites in whose land you now live? But as for me and my family, we will serve the LORD."

- Joshua 24:15

We can get insight into the meaning of salvation by doing a quick deep dive into the Greek meaning of the word salvation.

Salvation is translated *soteria* or *sozo* in Greek. *Sozo* means to save, rescue, deliver from danger, destruction, harm, ruin, or loss, while *soteria* means restoration to a state of safety, soundness, health and wellbeing as well as preservation from danger or destruction.

Salvation is therefore defined as wellness, wholeness, and saving of all parts of who we are—our spirit, soul, and body—from deterioration or death.

The second law of thermodynamics states that "in any closed system, a process proceeds in a direction such that entropy increases." In other words, over time, life is tending towards entropy, disorder, and destruction. We see this in our world with global warning and in our bodies. As we grow older, our bodies undergo natural wear and tear until the point of old age and eventual death. Based on this, we are all in need of salvation in many aspects of our lives to reverse or interrupt our inevitable path towards entropy.

Salvation of their spirit

Your spirit man is the unseen part of you that connects to God, who is spirit. Death simply means separation. When one's spirits separate from their body, they are dead. Similarly, a person is spiritually dead when their spirits are disconnected from God. Salvation in your spirit awakens your spirit from death and enables you to become aware of who God is and enter a relationship with Him. This is what the bible describes as 'eternal life'.

A person can be spiritual, that is, they are aware of, connect with, and take part in spiritual activity, but still be spiritually dead if they are not connected to the one true God.

In a world where we have so many "truths," religions, and claims about who God is, all contradicting each other, it is important that you pray for yourself, your children and loved ones, that you navigate through the plethora of information and come to the truth about God and salvation.

I have come to the realisation through research and personal encounter that we are saved in our spirit by coming into a relationship with Father God through His son Jesus Christ. If any of you are in doubt or disagree about the means of salvation, I love you and I pray for you that God will lead you and your children along the path of truth. I am more than willing to share evidence and answer questions that point to who the true God is. I do highly suggest you pray a prayer to the true God to reveal himself to you and He certainly will.

Salvation of their soul

The soul seats the will, emotions, thoughts, and knowledge of a person. Your soul is the portal through which realities in the spirit and physical realm become your own reality through knowledge, enlightenment, and thought patterns. A very popular scripture states, "be transformed by renewing your mind," meaning that change and transformation comes through a change, healing and salvation in the mind. Psychological and behavioural sciences use this principle in therapy, to change their client's behaviour and life outcomes through changing and healing the person's negative mindsets and programming.

Salvation of the soul occurs when your mind and thought patterns are healed from negative beliefs, memories, and experiences. This includes being aware of spiritual truths, solutions to needs or problems and creativity. It also involves healing your minds from brokenness, limiting beliefs and mental ill health, and healing our brain cells or any imbalances in your brain system.

Salvation and healing of their bodies

Salvation of the body refers to healing in our body and occurs when a person (1) walks in divine health that is to live sickness, infection and medication-free, (2) is healed from an ailment or illness, (3) is transformed into a perfect, sickness-free body at the end of the world when the Bible explains that all our bodies will be transformed, and death will not exist. I will go more in-depth about holistic healing of the spirit, soul, and body in my blog on myproverbs31family.com (search healing).3

Just as the opening text states, choose this day for you and your household. It's my prayer that you will choose the path of spiritual, psychological, and physical healing and salvation for you, your children and household. By taking part in this 31-day prayer challenge, you have already taken a step in the right direction, and I can't wait to hear your transformation stories!

Let us pray:

Scripture Recitation

Dear friend, I hope all is well with you and that you are as healthy in body as you are strong in spirit. Beloved, I pray that in every way you may prosper and enjoy good health, as your soul also prospers.

3 JOHN 1:2

For this is how God loved the world: He gave His one and only Son, so that everyone who believes in Him will not perish but have eternal life.

JOHN 3:16

And this is eternal life, that they know You, the only true God, and Jesus Christ whom You have sent.

JOHN 17:3

Jesus answered, "I am the way and the truth and the life. No one comes to the Father except through Me."

JOHN 14:6

Then I will sprinkle clean water on you, and you will be clean. Your filth will be washed away, and you will no longer worship idols. And I will give you a new heart, and I will put a new spirit in you. I will take out your stony (stubborn) heart (of unbelief) and give you a tender,(responsive, obedient) heart.

EZEKIEL 36:25-26

Prayers

1. Thank you, Lord, for Your precious gift of salvation for me and my household.

2. Thank you, Lord, for Your love for me and my children. For dying a painful death on the cross of Calvary so that my children and I will have salvation in spirit, soul, and body.

3. I pray that my children will have an encounter with God, and they will be fully assured of the truth of who You are, and Your will for salvation and healing for their lives.

4. Answer all doubts or questions they may have regarding salvation.

5. Wide is the path that leads to destruction, but narrow is the gate that leads to life.[41] May my children not follow the crowd or popular culture. May they not succumb to peer, political or media pressure, and political correctness but be led down the path that leads to life, light, and salvation.

6. Let my children's physical and spiritual eyes be open so that they can see and come to the truth of the gospel of Jesus Christ.

7. Let there be an outpouring of the Holy Spirit so that my children will grow and walk towards truth. Amid the plethora of deception, may they find truth. May only the truth about God and our Saviour Jesus be what makes sense to them.

8. I pray a blessing over their spirit. Let them have a spiritual encounter with Your precious Holy Spirit and may the dry bones of their spirit man come alive, in Jesus' name.

---

[41] Bible, Matthew 7:13

9. Like Samuel, may they hear the gentle knock of Jesus on the door of their hearts and may they open their hearts to Jesus.

10. I pray a blessing over their minds. May they be transformed and grow in godly wisdom, knowledge, and understanding. May they come to the truth of who God is. God's love and His purpose for them.

11. Help and remove their limiting beliefs and negative thoughts and ideas that prevent them from receiving salvation in their minds, spirits, and bodies.

12. May the love of and for God be shed abroad in the hearts of my children.

13. Thank you, Lord, that You have not given my children a spirit of fear but of love, joy, and a sound mind. May their minds be sound, full of love, joy, and truth.

14. Let Your will for sound health be done in their lives.

15. Thank you, that by the stripes and suffering of Jesus Christ, they are healed in spirit, soul, and body.

16. Lord, rebuke and expel the demons of sickness from my children, in Jesus' name.

17. Enable them to make lifestyle choices and disciplines that align with good health in their spirit, soul, and body.

18. Deliver them from the spiritual and mental arrows that fly by day, the terror by night, pestilence, viruses, and diseases. My children are protected by the blood of Jesus, and all sickness, viruses, and diseases will pass over them because of the divine protection of God.

19. Father, I thank You for answered Prayers.

Day 31

JOURNAL AND NOTES FOR CHILDREN

1. What are your goals and desires for being a better parent for your children?

2. What legacy, values, and behaviours do you want your children to adopt?

3. What is the Lord asking you to do/what actions will you take to meet your goals and manifest your desires for your children [put a date on each action]?

FINAL THOUGHTS

Thank you for making it to the end of this 31 days challenge. I am absolutely excited for what's about to happen in your life and marriage! Your life will never be the same as you repeat the Prayers and take the actions recommended in the book. Please leave a review on amazon or let me know how these 31 days have been for you. Be sure to go through and repeat the Prayers alone, with a partner, friend or group. It's also important to implement the actions recommended. You can do so by having an accountability partner or group. You are also very welcome to join my FREE proverbs 31 community where we will pray together and take part in challenges and activities that will help you manifest and nurture your purpose marriages. If you will like further support, or to talk through issues around purposeful dating, relationships or marriage, please don't hesitate to get in touch to book your free purpose call with me on: www.myproverbs31family/purposecall.

Don't Forget

As a thank you I will be sending you my Masterclass on How to Manifest your Purpose Marriage (plus other bonuses for my readers).

You will learn

- Why you don't have your purpose marriage yet?
- Why you have been waiting so long for what God promised you
- What you can do to manifest your purpose marriage

Access the course and many other bonuses:

www.myproverbs31family.com/POP31bonuses.

Before You Go

Thank you again for purchasing my book and reading all the way to the end. If you liked the book, take a minute or two to leave a review on Amazon so that other women just like you can find out about it.

Your feedback is most appreciated. Not only will it help me continue writing books like this and improve on it, but reviews are one of the ways by which more people will get to know about my book. Leave a review on amazon today: Thank you in advance!

Work With Swabrina

Swabrina is a dating, relationship and marriage preparation coach. She has helped many women around the world overcome negative relationship cycles, find purpose, increase their femininity, and proactively prepare for their purpose marriage. If you will like to get coaching support to address any of the relationship matters discussed in this book, schedule a FREE Purpose Consultation to get advice and discuss her coaching services to help you. Book now on: www.myproverbs31family/purposecall

Access free resources and your digital toolkit:

www.myproverbs31family/POP31bonuses .

For bulk orders of this book please contact

info@myproverbs31family.com for a generous discount schedule.

Hire Swabrina to speak at your events

www.myproverbs31family/speaking

Hire Swabrina to speak on topics covered in this book. Some topics around marriage preparation is listed below

Don't Wait- Purpose Driven Singles

1. How to overcome loneliness, depression and hopelessness but instead thrive while single
2. How to find purpose and live a purpose driven, profitable and fulfilled single life
3. How to overcome complacency but instead maximise the exclusive benefits of your single season
4. How to wait and prepare for purpose marriage proactively and productively

5. How to leave a legacy while single
6. The benefit and promise associated with pursuing purpose while single.

Feminine Foundations for preparing, attracting and keeping a passionate relationship

1. The evolution of femininity and masculinity and the impact of gender roles on relationship today
2. The importance of femininity in dating and relationships
3. How to balance your masculine and feminine energies as a modern-day successful woman
4. How to increase femininity in your dating and relationships

Navigating Dating in the 21st century as a woman of faith

1. The challenge of dating in the 21st century
2. Why many religious women are single and how religion has played a role in keeping women single
3. How organisations and churches can better support their single members
4. Pros and cons of dating
5. Pros and cons of the zero dating/supernatural method for manifesting marriage
6. How to date while keeping your purity and moral values

Arise And Shine- Turn your pain into purpose, and profit while single

1. How to identify your purpose and passion
2. How to turn your painful experiences into a profitable message
3. How to make an impact while single through writing and launching a course
4. Why your single season is the best time to write your book or launch your course
5. How to make profit and impact using your book while you are single
6. The secret benefit and promise of pursuing purpose, profit and impact while single

Printed in Great Britain
by Amazon